GREECE

An Illustrated History

GREECE

An Illustrated History

TOM STONE

HIPPOCRENE BOOKS, INC.
New York

Copyright© 2000 Tom Stone

ISBN 0-7818-0755-7

For information, address:
HIPPOCRENE BOOKS, INC.
171 Madison Avenue
New York, NY 10016

Cataloging-in-Publication Data available from the Library of Congress

Printed in the United States of America.

CONTENTS

INTRODUCTION

Greece is a country of improbable contrasts. In the north, bordering on the ever-simmering Balkans, it is wild, mountainous, forested and often savage, rife with game and dotted with heron-posted lakes and a plentiful network of rivers and streams. In the serene, sun-swept south, rock and marble predominate; bramble-covered hills are denuded of trees; the air is hot with the scent of oregano and thyme; and temples and churches blaze white against an azure sky.

It is a country of devout Byzantine Orthodox Christian worshippers who are revered by others for their classical, pagan past; a cradle of democracy whose history is characterized more by tyrannies, autocracies, despotism, foreign occupations, and military juntas than by freedom; a people who live in constant dread of foreign intrigues against their country, and yet are famous for their hospitality to foreigners; the birthplace of some of the most astute businesspeople the world has ever seen, but whose national economy continually threatens to collapse into Third World chaos; and a community that prides itself on patriotism yet deeply distrusts their fellow countrymen.

Much of this has to do with Greece's landscape. Perhaps the most momentous events of the distant Greek past, arguably more significant than either the Trojan War or the Minoan and Mycenaean civilizations, were those convulsions of the earth's crust that created the geography of Greece and would thus shape so much of the people's fiercely independent character and contentious, often self-divisive, history. These geological events occurred some 70 million years before human beings would wander onto the scene. A convergence of the Eurasian and African continental blocks pushed up the mountainous spine of the mainland, including the brooding mass of the Balkans in the north, and created a landscape much like a rolling sea. After the peaceful "Golden Age" of the Neolithic period, isolated islands of peoples clustered around this sea for protection — around a high point of land called an *acropolis* (in Greek, "high city") — and warily regarded all other communities as foreign, irrespective of similarities in language, social customs and religion.

In the same Cenozoic era, a subsequent pulling-apart of these continental blocks produced an additional fragmentation that opened the Bosphorus and sank the land mass between Greece proper and Asia Minor. Thus, the Greek archipelago was formed.

This scattering of some two thousand sea-linked mountaintops may provide a playground for tourists, but it has been an endless source of headaches for statesmen. For centuries they have engaged in fiery wrangling over which islands should properly belong to which continental block and whether there has ever been any real separation at all.

Political and geological aftershocks continue to be felt. Minor earth tremors are reported almost monthly in various parts of the country, and occasionally there are major earthquakes such as those that shook Corinth and Athens in 1986, devastated Kalamata in 1987, and struck the suburbs of Athens and Istanbul in 1999.

Internally, the country is as politically divided now as it was when the first wave of Greek-speaking peoples — known as "Hellenes" — arrived from the north in *c.* 2000 B.C. Not only does each change in national government bring about another round of vendettas against the previous administration and its followers, but inhabitants of the same island, living in villages only a few miles apart, habitually refer to the other villagers as *xénoi* ("foreigners" or "strangers").

As wary as the Greeks are of their own countrymen, other aspects of their geography make them even more suspicious of foreigners. In the north, Bulgaria and the former Yugoslavia have long coveted the thin strip of Greek land that separates their countries from the Aegean. Both the Balkan Wars of 1911–1914 and recent disputes over the name "Macedonia" reflect what Greeks see as a perpetual threat.

At the same time, disputes with Turkey over the territorial boundary between the latter's continental shelf and the Greek Aegean have kept the countries on a near war-footing for much of the past fifty years. As recently as 1996, active warfare nearly erupted when Turkish troops attempted to disembark on a group of rocks in the eastern Aegean.

But, in spite of all of these constant upheavals and seemingly irreconcilable contrasts, Greece maintains a unique identity. It is united by its songs, seas, dances, churches, heroes, and most of all, by its great leveling light — a light which sharply defines every pit and wrinkle of its multitudinous individuality, somehow binding it all together into that one single substance that Greeks from Thales to Kazantzakis have so longed for and celebrated.

PREHISTORIC GREECE

In prehistoric times, geological upheavals impeded easy over-
land access from both the north and the east. Therefore, it was not
until the Neolithic period that settlers began entering Greece in
significant numbers; most were farmers from Asia Minor, who
had traveled over the Bosphorus and across the Aegean.

Paleolithic and Neolithic Beginnings:
c. 500,000–6500 B.C.

Until the late 1980s, the earliest habitation of the Greek mainland was dated at *c.* 50,000 B.C. Current archaeological evidence
now indicates that Paleolithic peoples were living in caves at
Petralona, near Thessaloniki, as early as 500,000 B.C. Other similar sites can be found in the Vicos Gorge, on Lake Ioannina in
Epirus, and outside of Larissa in Thessaly.

The first major migrations into the Greek mainland and archipelago, however, did not occur until the beginning of the
Neolithic period (*c.* 6500 B.C.). Five hundred years later, there
were Neolithic settlements at Sesklo and Dimeni in Thessaly, and
in Corinth and Crete. These settlers did not speak Greek, and
their religion was likely centered on the Mother Goddess and the
continued fertility of the communities' crops and livestock. It was
during this period that worshipping began at Delphi, where a
gaseous cleft in the rocks became revered as the *ómphalos* or
"navel" of the world.

Delphi.

During the third millennium B.C., Neolithic communities spread throughout mainland Greece and were so developed in Crete that trade was established in Egypt and the Mediterranean. The first of many settlements appeared at Troy, on the northwestern Aegean coast of what is now Turkey. At the end of the millennium, Bronze Age weapons from Asia Minor first appeared in Greece.

In 2500 B.C., a "Great Deluge" occurred in Egypt and the Near East, which almost certainly inspired the Greek story of the flood of Deucalion and the Biblical tale of Noah. This catastrophe precipitated a second wave of migration into the area from the east. At about the same time, the first settlements at Mycenae and Tiryns were established, as was Cycladic culture in the central Greek islands. The first signs of what would become known as the Minoan civilization appeared on Crete.

Minoan and Mycenaean Civilizations: *c.* 2000–1200 B.C.

In the second millennium B.C., as the Minoan civilization evolved from its peaceful, goddess-worshipping Neolithic beginnings (there were no defensive fortifications at any of its centers, neither on Crete nor on the island of Santorini), the patriarchal warrior society that would eventually destroy it invaded the country from the north, leaving widespread destruction in its wake.

These peoples, who brought with them the Greek language and weapons and chariots, were collectively known as "Hellenes." (Hence, the Greek name for the country, *Helláda*, rather

3

A Minoan snake-goddess.

The Lion Gate at Mycenae.

than the Roman-derived appellation "Greece.") They invaded through the Balkans (*c.* 2000–1900 B.C.) and spread throughout the mainland, uprooting farm communities that had existed since Neolithic times. Among their various tribes was the Achaeans. Settling in the northeastern corner of the Peloponnese, they came to be known as Mycenaeans after the name of their principal center of power, Mycenae.

Meanwhile, on the safe and isolated island of Crete, Minoan civilization was flowering as the dominant sea power in the Aegean. By 1600 B.C., the palace of Knossos had been built. It was designed by the legendary architect and inventor Daedelus to house the bull-like offspring of the illicit liaison between Pasiphae and the taurean incarnation of the ever-amorous Cretan, Zeus.

While there was contact between the Minoans and the Mycenaeans (recorded in the latter's early Greek Linear B accounting notations), the Mycenaeans initially curbed their aggressive instincts towards Crete — that is, until a volcanic eruption at Santorini (also called Thira) irrevocably weakened the Minoans. While there is considerable disagreement among scholars as to the exact cause of the Cretan collapse, all agree that the force of the Santorini eruption *c.* 1500 B.C. (some seven times greater than that of Karakatoa in 1883) played a significant role. The palaces of Crete, including that at Knossos, were burned and destroyed some fifty years later; by that time, the Mycenaeans had become the dominant power in the area.

Bronze statue of Poseidon or Zeus, at the Athens National Museum (460–450 B.C.).

Greece's "Heroic Age": *c.* 1500–1200 B.C.

Greece's Heroic Age lasted from the Mycenaeans' ascension to power to their collapse under the onslaught of yet another wave of invaders from the north: the Dorians.

From 1400 B.C. to 1200 B.C., the Mycenaeans controlled all of southern mainland Greece and the Aegean, from Crete in the west to Cyprus in the east. A warrior civilization, its centers of power were massive, walled citadels perched on commanding heights, such as those found in Mycenae and the acropolis of Athens. (Athens was traditionally founded in 1582 B.C. with the aid of the goddess Athena.)

During this same period, Cadmus founded Thebes (*c.* 1300 B.C.) and Pelops settled the Peloponnese (1280 B.C.), hence the peninsula's name, "Island of Pelops."

The extent of the Mycenaeans' power is demonstrated by recorded raids on Egypt and the Hittite Empire in central Turkey, where they were most probably the "Sea Peoples" held responsible for that empire's eventual downfall.

In 1250 B.C., there was an explosion of legendary activity: Jason and the Argonauts' pursuit of the Golden Fleece; Oedipus' journey to Thebes; Theseus' travels from Athens to Crete and back again, confronting the Minotaur and abandoning Ariadne on Naxos; Daedelus' design of the labyrinth, and his son Icarus' attempt to fly on the wings of wax his father had invented; and, the unfolding of tragic events told in the tales of Phaedra and Medea.

The Trojan War occurred *c.* 1225 B.C., spawning its own legends of Odysseus and Aeneas and the tragedies of the house of Atreus, including Agamemnon, Clytemnestra, Electra, and

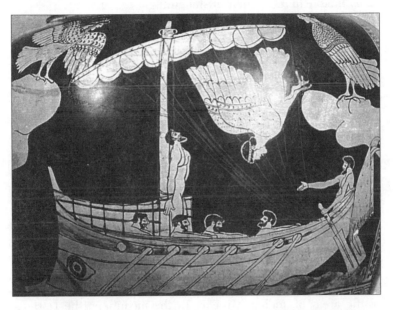

Red-figure vase depicting Odysseus being tempted by the Sirens.

Orestes. Meanwhile, the ten-year siege of Troy had greatly weakened Mycenaean power in the region. By the time the Dorians invaded from the north a century later, the Mycenaeans were virtually unable to resist their onslaught.

The Dorians: *c.* 1200–1000 B.C.

The Dorians were Greek-speaking and even more war-like than the Mycenaeans. Their weapons of forged iron gave them a devastating advantage over the bronze implements of the Mycenaeans. Over the course of the next two hundred years, the Dorians gradually gained hegemony over virtually all of mainland Greece and the Aegean islands. On the mainland, only the fortifications on the Athenian acropolis remained unconquered, while those of Mycenae were completely destroyed.

The Mycenaeans fled to the islands and then to the coast of Turkey, where they founded Ephesus in 1000 B.C. Their presence there would eventually create one of the great cultural and scientific areas of ancient Greece. In the meantime, the Dorians established the great cities of Corinth (1100 B.C.) and Sparta (1000 B.C.). They wanted to ensure that their gods — those of Mt. Olympus — would replace all vestiges of the Great Mother and the various Chthonic deities of the Mycenaeans. The Dorian myth of the return of the prodigal Hercules (a Dorian) to Thebes established the legitimacy of their takeover.

The Dark Ages: *c.* 1000-800 B.C.

The two hundred years that followed the Dorian invasion were ones of massive realignment — migrations, resettlements, and subjugations — that left no written records. When the smoke and confusion finally cleared, the former Mycenaean aristocracies had merged with the communal and more egalitarian social order of the Dorian and the various tribal villages to create a basis for Greek city-states. These were the first glimmerings of Greek "democracy."

The Dark Ages finally ended in 776 B.C., when the first games between city-states were established at Olympia. The recording of these dates at four-year intervals brought the undated prehistory of Greece to an end.

As the Dark Ages receded, Greek writing, based on the Phoenician alphabet, replaced Mycenaean script in business accounting and in poetry; in art, human beings were depicted on pottery for the first time; and in literature, Hesiod wrote not only the first systematic treatment of the new Greek gods, the *Theogeny*, but a moral examination of life among the mortals, *Works and Days*. In Ionia, on the coast of Asia Minor, the works of Homer (*c.* 850–650 B.C.) were written down for the first time.

ARCHAIC GREECE: *c.* 800–500 B.C.

Archaic Greece was marked by the continuing political development of the Greek city-state or *polis* — particularly in Corinth, Athens, and Sparta — and by the expansion of these city-states' power into colonies around the Aegean and the Black Sea. In Ionia, contact with the highly-developed Lydian and Persian civilizations brought about a fertilization of Greek art and thought that would eventually lead to the great flowering of accomplishments that marked Greece's Golden Age in fifth-century B.C. Athens.

For most of the eighth century B.C., the Euboean cities of Chalkis and Eretria were among the predominant powers in Greece. In 800 B.C., they founded the first trading base in the Middle East: Al Mina, on the Orontes River in northern Syria. It was perhaps here that they acquired the Phoenician alphabet that would become the basis of post-Mycenaean written Greek. At about the same time, they also established a "new city" (*neopólis*), Naples, in southern Italy.

Over the next fifty years, the Euboeans and other Greek city-states — Sparta, Corinth, Achaia, Crete, and Rhodes — colonized Sicily and southern Italy, which came to be called *Magna Graecia* ("Greater Greece") by the Romans.

A territorial dispute between Eretria and Chalkis in 734 B.C. erupted into a war that gradually engulfed most other city-states. Called the Lelantine War, and lasting until 680 B.C., it resulted in the complete dissolution of Euboean power in Greece.

During this period, both Sparta and Athens moved towards the establishment of hegemony over their regions, the Peloponnese and Attica respectively, and the formation of their disparate political systems. In 700 B.C., under Lycurgus, the Spartans adopted a form of government that gave minimum rights to Sparta's citizen-soldiers but preserved the ruling oligarchy's power and its hereditary kingship. Athens replaced its hereditary kingship in 683 B.C. with a rule of *árchons* elected by peers from the *areopágus*, a council of aristocrats. Neither city-state bestowed great power on the people, however, and this neglect resulted in an increasing restlessness among the populace and the rise of tyrannies in various city-states throughout Greece.

The Ionian civilization continued to flower, particularly at its great religious center of Ephesus and its booming port and cultural capital of Miletus.

The Tyrannies

Tyrannos ("tyrant") is a non-Greek word that was first applied to Gyges of Lydia (680–648 B.C.). There is a difference of opinion as to whether the term originally possessed the same negative connotation as it does today. The fact that the Greeks did not invent a word for the phenomenon in their own language is thought to mean that they considered it to be something foreign and therefore negative. On the other hand, *tyrannos* was understood by a majority of the Greek people to be the kind of government established by strong individuals who were concerned with granting some rights and better civic conditions to the rising middle classes. It thus enjoyed widespread approval, at least initially. A century later, however, in his fable, *The Wolf and the Lamb*, Aesop would say: "Any excuse will serve a tyrant."

In 655 B.C., Greece's first recorded tyrant, Kypselos, overthrew the ruling Dorian clan at Corinth and, with his son Periander, established an autocracy that would last until 585 B.C. They soon made Corinth one of the great powers in the area. Kypselos' success was followed by various other attempts at tyrannies, including that of Theagenes at Megara. However, not all would-be tyrants were as successful. Theagenes' aristocratic son-in-law, for example, seized the Acropolis only to be thwarted by the peasants he was purporting to liberate. In 621 B.C., Theagenes provoked the Athenian *árchon*, Dracos, to issue the famously harsh laws that were designed to pre-empt such actions.

These "Draconian measures," the city-state's first written laws, firmly codified the separation of rights between rich landowners and merchants on the one hand, and serfs and slaves on the other. In so doing, they made a large number of crimes punishable by death.

Twenty-five years later (594 B.C.), the Athenian magistrate Solon was elected chief *árchon* and attempted to mollify the continuing unrest of the populace by introducing radical social and political changes. He canceled all debts, guaranteed freedom from slavery for debt, created a People's Council as the ultimate court of law, and gave a measure of political power to all four social classes.

But this would not be enough. After Solon retired, a second attempt at establishing a tyranny succeeded in 561 B.C. Its leader was the Athenian general, Peisistratus, who had allied himself with upland farmers against the conservatives and liberals who supported Solon's constitution.

Peisistratus' reign and that of his sons, Hippias and Hipparchus, would last until 510 B.C., but was not without its ups and downs. The Athenian aristocracy would overthrow Peisistratus twice before he firmly consolidated his power, most memorably re-establishing his tyranny by marching on the Acropolis in 550 B.C. dressed as the goddess Athena.

In the meantime, Sparta had extended its more egalitarian rule throughout the Peloponnese, after having quelled a prolonged revolt (650-630 B.C.) of Messenian slaves; and, in 560 B.C., it formed the Peloponnesian League, an alliance of most of the major power centers in the area except Argos and Archaea. This league lasted until 380 B.C. and was instrumental in the defeat of Athens in the Peloponnesian Wars of the fifth century B.C.

In the same era, the Ionian tyrant, Thrasybolus, presided over and successfully preserved the independence, economic power, and cultural blossoming of the port of Miletus. In the other power center of the Greek world, Corinth, Periander became a tyrant.

The Lydians and Persians

While Athens and Sparta evolved their increasingly different forms of government, the Lydians and Persians consolidated their power on the Asian continent, eyeing both one another and Greece to the west. By 560 B.C., Lydia's King Alyattes and his son, Croesus, had subjugated the entire Greek Ionian coast except for Miletus. At the same time, Cyrus II was just ascending the throne in Persia and beginning a consolidation of power that would lead to the establishment of the Persian Empire.

Cyrus defeated Croesus at Sardis in 545 B.C., putting an end to the Lydian Empire and imposing Persian hegemony over Ionia. He installed loyal Greek tyrants in its cities and concluded an alliance with the still-unconquered Miletus. Instead of using this territory to launch an invasion of the Greek mainland, however, Cyrus turned his attention towards insurgents near his home territory. In 529 B.C., he was killed during a battle in eastern Iran. His son-in-law, Darius I, succeeded him in 521 B.C.

Nine years later, after campaigns in Egypt and India, Darius crossed the Bosphorus into Thrace and began his near-legendary effort to add Greece and the regions of the lower Danube to his burgeoning empire.

The Arts and Sciences

With the end of the Dark Ages in Greece and the beginning of contact with other civilizations, most significantly in the east, there was a blossoming of Greek arts and sciences. This impressively foreshadowed the sudden emergence of the Renaissance out of the Middle Ages two thousand years later — a cultural "rebirth" whose humanism had fittingly been sown in Greece during the period now under consideration.

Literature

The plying of merchant ships between Greece and the Middle East in the latter half of the eighth century B.C. resulted in the acquisition and adaptation of the Phoenician alphabet to the original

Greek language. (Heretofore it had been transcribed in a rudimentary cuneiform of the kind found inscribed in the Linear B tablets at Mycenae.) With this ability both to copy down oral works of literature and to express personal opinions and emotions to an enduring audience — to, in effect, immortalize the history of one's time, one's tribe, and one's self — literary activities proliferated and likely engendered similar anthropocentric efforts not only in the arts but in the sciences as well. Man became the subject in both senses of the word: an observer and measurer of the universe, and an object of investigation within it.

Among the first, if not the first, poetic works to be transcribed with the new alphabet were those of Homer. Although scholars still dispute the evidence, it is possible that Homer himself did the transcribing. Born in Ionia between 800–750 B.C., during the period when spoken Greek was being adapted to the Phoenician alphabet, Homer may have grown up with the ability to record his own works. In any case, by the time third-century Greek scholars began work on a standardized text of the poem for the library at Alexandria, there were numerous and very different versions of Homer's epic in circulation — all copies of crumbled papyrus copies, a *Rashomon* of personal interpretations that had been passed down through the centuries.

A contemporary of Homer, Hesiod was born in Boetia on the Greek mainland, where, as noted above, he composed the first written record of Greek mythology, the *Theogeny*, as well as *Works and Days*, a moral treatise on the virtues of hard work and proper behavior.

The colonizer and soldier, Archilochus of Paros, created what is considered to be the first truly personal lyric poetry in

17

Linear B tablets found at Knossos.

670 B.C., adding his own deeply felt thoughts to a genre previously thought of as mere words sung to the accompaniment of a lyre. Some sixty years later, Sappho, along with Alcaeus of Lesbos, would raise the form to high art, setting the bar for future lyricists. The poet Pindar of Thebes (*c.* 502 B.C.) would make a career of performing his own poetry and music before various Grecian courts, including that of Alexander I of Macedonia.

About the time of Sappho, a freed Phrygian slave by the name of Aesop embarked on a peripatetic career as a teller of his own tales: a set of moralizing fables that he dispensed with great success throughout Greece and Persia — that is, until he reached the shrine at Delphi. The oracle's priests, angered at Aesop's effrontery, planted one of the shrine's golden cups in his baggage and then accused him of stealing it. As punishment, he was thrown off a cliff to his death.

The Visual Arts

In the visual arts, the traditional abstract style of geometric pottery design was gradually becoming more pictorial and humanistic. During the latter part of the seventh century B.C., early Corinthian pottery began to include not only a universe of plants, animals, and legendary beasts, but human beings as well — largely, men in Homeric scenes. At approximately the same time, the production of Attic black figure pottery began at Keramicus in Athens, and it soon became the dominant influence in Greece. Masters of this form include Clitias, Execias, and Ergotimus, maker of the astonishing "Vase of François" (now in Florence).

Around 625 B.C., the first large statues of men and women appeared: monumental figures of nude male youths (singular: *koúros*), and clothed maidens (singular: *kóre*) at temple sanctuaries and gravesites. The former perhaps celebrated athletic feats, while the latter may have been testaments of grief over premature deaths. Though the stiffness of their posture betrays an Egyptian influence, these statues' abstract impassiveness allows them to symbolize all men and women, rather than, as in the Egyptian case, a specific prince or god. Thus, the worshippers gazing upon these statues were made aware of the divine and eternal that resided within every human being.

This was also becoming apparent in changes to the ritual "goat song" dances that celebrated the cult of Dionysos. Originally, these village rituals featured choral singing and dancing and a blood sacrifice of goats to the wine god. However, at the first Athens Dionysia festival in 535 B.C., the poet and dramatist Thespis separated himself from the chorus and became the first actor: a solo, priest-like "responder" who narrated the birth, passion, and rebirth of the god in between choral odes. While not yet a protagonist, this single performer was the first real step towards turning a religious ceremony into a human drama.

This period also saw temples built for the worship of those gods and goddesses whose divinity was believed to be embodied in cult statues. The architectural styles of these temples gradually evolved into the roofed Doric order of the Greek mainland, the Ionian order from the coast of Asia Minor, and the later Corinthian order emerging from the city-state of Corinth. Sanctuaries built during the sixth century B.C. include: the first major temple to Athena in Athens (583 B.C.); a new temple at Delphi by the Athenian aristocratic dynasty, the Alkmeonids (548 B.C.); and the temple of Artemis at Ephesus in Ionia (*c.* 540 B.C.), one of the seven wonders of the ancient world.

Near the end of the Archaic period (*c.* 525 B.C.), the technique for red-figure vase painting was invented in Athens. Masters of this form include Euphronias (the *krater* of Hercules wrestling with Anteus) and Sosias (the vase of Achilles and Patroclus).

The temple of Apollo at Corinth with its high city (acropolis) in the background.

A red-figure vase showing Achilles dragging Hector's body around the walls of Troy.

The Sciences and Philosophy

During the seventh and sixth centuries B.C., science and philosophy developed almost inseparably as inquiries into the nature of the universe and man's place in it. At the center of these investigations was Miletus, a wealthy seaport that remained the lone autonomous city after the Lydian subjugation of Ionia. Legend has it that the city's bid for independence was aided considerably by a young Milesian named Thales, who helped the Lydian king win a major battle by correctly predicting a solar eclipse (*c.* 582). Whether or not this happened, Thales certainly did exist and was responsible for establishing the first school of philosophy and science in the Western world. Handing down the example of a lively, inquiring mind to his pupils, he brought world theorizing out of the realm of myth, religion, legend, and poetry and into the rational human mind.

One of Thales' principal concerns was the discovery of a primary substance from which all things were made. After considerable observation and "scientific" investigation, he conjectured that this original matter was water, because it was able to become both a gas and a solid. His brilliant pupil, Anaximander, continued Thales' investigations and added accomplishments of his own, such as the creation of the first maps ever made in the West. Anaximander also formulated the first concepts of matter, evolution, and the creation of the universe. He postulated a plurality of worlds and theorized that the primary substance was an "Indefinite Something" out of which pairs of opposites are formed, with the interaction between the pairs continuing the ferment of being and becoming. In turn, his pupil Anaximenes theorized that the primary substance was vapor or air — from which our world arose through the process of condensation and rarefaction — and that the differences between things and substances were due to their differing degrees of expansion or compression.

In 521 B.C., Darius I took power in Persia and began to create his great empire. Contemporaneously, three other major philosophers surfaced in the Ionian area.

The first was Anaximenes' pupil, the reformist poet and philosopher Xenophones of Kolophon (c. 570–475 B.C.), who attacked the conventional theology of Homer and Hesiod and asserted the existence of a supreme god who was also the basic substance of the universe. At the beginning of his long career (he lived to be ninety), Xenophones emigrated to Sicily and the court of Hiero — a signal of what would become a definite shift of the center of Greek philosophical inquiry from Ionia westward to southern Italy, Sicily, and Athens.

The second was the philosopher and mystic Pythagoras, who moved from Samos to Crotona (Italy), where he established a school called the Pythagorean Brotherhood; he coined the term "philosopher, friend (*feélos*) of wisdom (*sophós*)," and postulated the theory that all things in the universe are ultimately reducible to numbers.

The third, Heracleitus of Ephesus, dealt with the problem of change in the primary substance, and stated that everything was in the process of becoming. He postulated fire as the basic material of the universe, in which there is, and will be, an identity of opposites. "Nothing," he is reported to have said, "is permanent except change."

And change was certainly in the air as the sixth century B.C. ended, and the fifth century began.

The Persian king, Darius.

THE PERSIAN WARS

In 494 B.C., after a plan to single-handedly gain control of the southern Aegean collapsed, the Milesian tyrant Aristagoras stirred up a revolt of Ionian cities against Darius I and the Persians. He was eventually aided by Athens, which needed to protect its trade routes to the Black Sea from Persian encroachment, and Eretria, which honored an old alliance with Miletus. Sparta was also invited but declined, preferring not to send its forces so far from home. The Greeks captured and burned Sardis, the Persian capital, but the tide soon turned. The Athenians at Ephesus retreated to the Greek mainland after being attacked by Darius, who then sacked and burned the abandoned city. Having effectively ended Ephesus' importance as an economic and cultural power, Darius made plans to invade Greece and avenge himself on Athens and Eretria.

While attempting to invade Greece from the Hellespont a year later (493 B.C.), Darius' fleet was destroyed by a storm off the peninsula of present-day Mt. Athos. In 490 B.C., a new Persian fleet landed on Euboea with one hundred thousand men and destroyed Eretria; it then crossed Attica to Marathon, likely aided by the former Athenian tyrant Hippias, whose father, Peisistratus, had once fought a successful battle there.

At the Battle of Marathon, the Greek general Miltiades led a small force of ten thousand men (including Aeschylus) and defeated the Persians by means of superior tactics. Following the victory, the Greek long-distance runner Phidippides raced 42.2 kilometers back to a surprised and a jubilant Athens with the

The helmet of Miltiades.

news, and made the marathon journey more famous, perhaps, than the battle itself.

With Sparta arriving too late to join in the triumph, and the Persian fleet beating an ignominious retreat to the Ionian coast, Athens was now regarded as the savior of Greece. But the Persians were far from finished.

Upon Darius' death in 485 B.C., his son, Xerxes I, promptly began an extensive four-year preparation to reinvade Greece. He assembled the world's largest army, built bridges of boats across the Hellespont (i.e. the Bosphorus), and dug a canal through the peninsula of present-day Mt. Athos — all of this in order to avoid the bad weather that had thwarted his father's invasion.

During this period of preparation, however, the Athenians discovered a rich vein of silver in mines near Sounion, and they built a new fleet of two hundred triremes at Themistocles' urging. Themistocles, elected *árchon* in 493 B.C., had already been instrumental in the creation of an Athenian port at Piraeus, ten miles to the west.

In 481 B.C., most of the city-states in Greece met at Corinth and, in a rare display of unity, formed what is now known as the Hellenic League in order to combat the imminent Persian invasion. After a long debate, it was decided that a force would be sent north to block the Persians before they could reach Attica and Athens.

In May of 480 B.C., Xerxes' army of approximately two hundred thousand men took one week to cross the Hellespont bridges. It then marched across the length of Thrace and Macedonia to meet the Persian navy, which had sailed through the Mt. Athos canal and was waiting in the Bay of Thermi (i.e. Thessaloniki).

Themistocles.

In August, the Spartan king Leonidas led a now-legendary force of three hundred Spartans who knowingly sacrificed their lives to delay the Persian advance at the pass of Themopylae. This action forced the Persian fleet to sail towards Athens in the dangerous open waters around Euboea, and allowed the Athenians to evacuate their capital and regroup their naval forces in the narrow waters of the Bay of Salamis. When Xerxes finally arrived in Athens, he and his army sacked the deserted city, destroying its walls and the buildings on the Acropolis.

In September, the Athenian fleet was still awaiting the Persians in the Bay of Salamis. With winter looming, Xerxes decided to attack the Athenians, despite the fact that there was little room there for his larger ships and fleet to maneuver. With Xerxes watching, reportedly from a golden throne on a nearby hillside, the opposing ships jammed together; the Greeks boarded the Persians' ships and emerged victorious due to a much superior infantry. Most of the Persian army and remaining fleet subsequently withdrew to Asia Minor.

At about the same time as the battle of Salamis (tradition says the same day), the Sicilian Greeks destroyed the Etruscan fleet at the Battle of Himera; the playwright Euripides was born on Salamis; and Sophocles participated as a boy dancer in the victory celebration.

In the spring of 479 B.C., the Persian army returned and once more forced the Athenians to evacuate their capital. When the expected Spartans finally arrived, the Persians awaited them on the plain of Plataia in Boiotia. In August, a combined Greek force led by the Spartan commander Pausanias engaged the Persians in the Battle of Plataia. After several weeks of fighting, Spartan hoplites stormed the Persian camp and slaughtered virtually all of its occupants.

At approximately the same time, a Greek expeditionary force caught the Persian fleet beached just off the Ionian coast at Mycale, and annihilated it. The two victories not only ended all possibility of a subsequent Persian invasion, but, for the contemporary historian Herodotus and his fellow Athenians, definitively proved the superiority of democracy over the autocratic despotism practiced by the Eastern "barbarians."

An aerial view of the Bay of Salamis where the Greeks defeated the Persians in 479 B.C.

CLASSICAL GREECE:
THE FIFTH CENTURY B.C.

Athens' rise to predominance in the Aegean initiated Greece's Classical period — a Golden Periclean Age of literature, art, science, philosophy, and politics bracketed by two devastating Peloponnesian Wars. The Classical period ended with Athenian democracy tottering on the bloodied knife-edge of totalitarianism, and with Socrates condemned to death for speaking his mind.

Following the defeat of the Persians, Themistocles ordered the immediate rebuilding of Athenian fortifications, despite Spartan objections that they were not necessary in peacetime.

Two years later, in 477 B.C., Athens established the Delian League with the city-states of Ionia as a defense against future Persian attacks. According to the agreement, Athens contributed only sea power and controlled the treasury on the island of Delos, where the tributes of the other members were deposited. This money, plus its huge navy and rebuilt fortifications, made Athens the dominant power in Greece and effectually created an Athenian Empire.

With this empire came excesses of power and imperialism that today are often overlooked in the glow of other Golden Age accomplishments. Athens compelled other Grecian city-states to join the alliance with its unchallenged naval superiority — all in hope of establishing hegemony over the entire Aegean, except for that part controlled by Sparta and its Peloponnesian League.

In 471 B.C., Themistocles was ostracized, justly or unjustly, for embezzling public funds. The Spartan Pausinias then accused Themistocles of treachery, implicating him in a plot to make Sparta and the rest of Greece subject to the Persians. Summoned to an Athenian trial, Themistocles sought refuge in Persia, where Xerxes appointed him regent of Magnesia.

Two years later, Kimon of Athens defeated the Persians at Eurymedon River in southeast Asia Minor. With the Persian threat thereby eradicated, Athens was free to impose its will on any of the Greek city-states who objected to joining the Delian League.

After the island of Naxos attempted to secede from the Delian League, Athenian-led League forces blockaded the island in 467 B.C. and forced it to reassume its membership. This action set a precedent for the League in acting against one of its own allies.

Under a secret pact with the Spartans, the island of Thasos was the next member to revolt against the alliance. But the Spartans, beset by problems at home, were unable to honor their commitment, and Athens crushed the revolt.

Shortly after that, in 464 B.C., Sparta suffered further difficulties: a catastrophic earthquake; a revolt of the "helots," a subjugated people used by the Spartans as slaves; and a third war against the subjugated Messenians to the west.

Under the alliance of 481 B.C., the Spartans asked Athens for assistance against the Messenians. Kimon, now the leading influence in the assembly, agreed to send an army. But the Spartans did an about-face and asked the Athenians to leave, apparently fearful that they might end up joining the Messenians in an alliance against Sparta.

This rejection of Kimon's army began a series of events that would topple the pro-Spartan faction in the Athenian Assembly and put what were then called the "radical" Democrats in power. These men would sow the seeds for the great Athenian classical age, its ultimate destruction by Sparta, and its subsequent degeneration into totalitarian rule.

In 461 B.C., at the instigation of Pericles, Kimon was ostracized for having Spartan sympathies. Ephialtes subsequently gained senate leadership for the Democratic Party; together with Pericles, he stripped the *Areopágus* (the ancient senate) of all but its basic judicial powers and relegated the *árchons* to chief judges. The Democrats then abolished Athens' alliance with Sparta and made new alliances with pro-Persian Thessaly and with Argos, Sparta's neighbor and bitter enemy.

When Ephialtes was assassinated by an agent of the oligarchy, the leadership of the democratic party fell to Pericles, son of the Persian war hero Xanthippus. At the time of his ascendancy, Pericles was thirty-three years old.

The First Peloponnesian War

The war is so called not because it took place in the Peloponnese, but because it was a confrontation between Athens and the entire Peloponnesian League, or Peloponnesians. In addition, an Athenian general, Thucydides (*c.* 460–400 B.C.), wrote its history.

It should be noted that Pericles was not at the head of government. He was an annually-elected general and, as such, was solely responsible for executing whatever policy was decided

Pericles.

upon by the Athenian Assembly as a whole. Certainly, he had the right to address the assembly and try to influence its decision, but so did every single one of Athens' seven thousand citizens. With that said, Pericles was such a brilliant orator, general, statesman, and leader that his wishes were near commands.

In 460 B.C., at about the time of Pericles' assumption of the democratic faction's leadership, the assembly authorized the construction of "Long Walls" from Athens to the port of Piraeus — a distance of ten miles, making it the country's largest and strongest fortress. The Athenians further antagonized Sparta by helping insurgent Messenians and helots find refuge in Naupaktos, and by continuously extending Athens' sphere of influence throughout the country and into Egypt.

After a territorial dispute with Corinth, Megara defected from the Peloponnesian League to Athens in 457–456 B.C.; in return for its assistance, Athens received a base in Megara.

These concrete threats to the balance of power between the Delian League and the Peloponnesian League prompted the Spartans and Corinthians to send troops to prevent Athenian expansion into the area north of Attica. This preemptive act sparked the first Peloponnesian War.

In a battle at Tanagra in Thessaly, the Spartans badly beat the Athenians, but departed the region immediately afterwards due to heavy losses. Thus, the field was left free for Athens to gain hegemony over central Greece, from Attica north to Thermopylae. Meanwhile, the island of Aegina was forcibly absorbed into the Delian League, and the Long Walls were completed.

Athenian ships circled the Peloponnese in 455 B.C., burning the naval base of Gythion, attacking other bases in the Gulf of

Corinth, and establishing a permanent fortress at the Gulf of Pegae. That same year, however, the Persians and Egyptians destroyed a large Athenian invasion fleet anchored in the Nile delta — an event that severely crippled Athenian sea power and led to the transfer of the Delian treasury to Athens for security.

Sparta and Athens, both needing to recover from respective heavy losses, agreed to a five-year armistice in 451 B.C. Two years later, as Themistocles died in Persian exile, a peace treaty with Persia coincidentally followed, under which the Aegean Sea was recognized as Greek territory.

In 448 B.C., Pericles proposed a pan-Hellenic peace conference at Athens to discuss Persian tributes and the rebuilding of shrines they had destroyed during the invasion. In spite of the armistice, Sparta refused to attend the conference on grounds that both the venue and the Athenian shrines under discussion would merely strengthen Athens' prestige. Other city-states agreed with Sparta, and the conference was scuttled. Nevertheless, the Delian League was gradually transformed into an Athenian Empire; tribute payments continued to finance Pericles' vision of Athens as Greece's cultural center.

Boiotia, bordering Attica to the north, revolted in 447 B.C. Ignoring Pericles' advice, the Athenian Assembly immediately sent troops. These were routed and Athens was subsequently forced to recognize Boiotian independence and withdraw its claim to recent gained land in central Greece. Killed in this battle was the father of Alcibiades, who then became Pericles' ward.

But Pericles' vision of an Athenian Golden Age continued unabated, as witnessed by the construction of the Parthenon on the Acropolis from 447 to 438 B.C. Its architects were Iktinos and Kallitkrates, and its sculptor was Pheidias. The Parthenon was remarkable, among many other things, for its inclusion of the first Corinthian columns.

Part of the frieze from the Parthenon showing Poseidon, Apollo, and Artemis.

In 446 B.C., the Attica-flanking states of Euboea and Megara seceded from the Athenian alliance. With Athenian troops thus preoccupied, a Peloponnesian army invaded Attica. But reaching as far as Eleusis, the army inexplicably turned back, perhaps with the Periclean promise of a substantial annual sum for having retreated. Subsequently, the Athenians suppressed the Euboean revolt and occupied Megara.

Athens and Sparta agreed to The Thirty Years' Peace in 445 B.C., under which Athens withdrew from Megara and recognized Spartan hegemony in the Peloponnese. In turn, Sparta recognized Athens' naval empire.

However, it was definitely a cold war and, with tensions continuing, the peace would last only fourteen years.

Arts and Sciences in the Early Classical Period

Paradoxically, the destruction of Athens during its victory over the Persians was a great impetus for the arts, as it cleared the ground for the rebuilding of the magnificent city and provided pride, self-confidence, and heroic subject matter for Greek artisans — poets, emerging playwrights, painters, sculptors, and architects.

Pindar

In the beginning of the Classical Period, the major poet was Pindar (518–442 B.C.). With peace both abroad and within greater Greece, the four major Panhellenic Games resumed.

Pindar's commissioned composition of lyric songs ("odes") to commemorate the victors at these games made him wealthy and famous. Later, his odes became the models for those of, among others, Milton, Grey, Goethe, Wordsworth, and Shelley.

Aeschylus

With the Festival of Dionysios, the Dionysia, once more alive at Athens, there emerged the first of Athens' great triad of tragic playwrights, Aeschylus (*c.* 524–456 B.C.). Although he had had his first play produced at the festival in 499 B.C., it was not until 484 B.C. that he took the prize. After fighting as an infantryman in the decisive victory over the Persians at Salamis, he took second place with a play, *The Persians*, honoring that battle.

In the course of his career, Aeschylus introduced several important new elements into drama: a second actor (later adding a third, following the lead of the young Sophocles); spectacle in the form of painted scenery and the machinery of the *deus ex machina*, capable of lowering gods and ghosts from above; and elevated shoes to increase the performers' stature. An accomplished musician, he also included music (flute solos) and dancing in his productions. But his main contribution was a shift from a poetic recounting of events to a dramatic depiction of them as if they were actually happening.

The greatest of Aeschylus' works — *Agamemnon*, *The Libation Bearers*, and *The Eumenides* — comprise the only surviving trilogy of classical times, the *Oresteia*, which won him the last of his thirteen prizes in 458 B.C. But, as a conservative from an aristocratic land-owning family, he had become deeply disillusioned

Aeschylus' Eumenides; *vase scene by Python (c. 350–340 B.C.).*

41

by the democratic reforms of Ephialtes and Pericles, particularly the stripping of the *Areopágus* (which Aeschylus exalted in *The Eumenides*) of its accumulated powers. Aeschylus moved to Sicily and died there in 456 B.C., at the age of sixty-nine, when an eagle purportedly dropped a tortoise on his bald head, mistaking it for a rock.

In his self-composed epitaph there was no mention of his plays. Rather, he wished to be remembered for his "fighting prowess" at Marathon against the Persians.

Sophocles

Sophocles (*c.* 496–406 B.C.) was born at Colonus, on the outskirts of Athens. At age sixteen, he was picked to lead the chorus of young men who celebrated the defeat of the Persians at Salamis. Later, he became a well-known actor, but decided on a career as a tragic playwright. Becoming one of Athens' greatest, Sophocles is said to have written some one hundred and twenty-three plays and never to have placed worse than second in any competition.

Like Aeschylus, Sophocles was a military man, twice an elected general and serving in two campaigns: with Pericles during the Samian War, and with Nikias during the Peloponnesian Wars. In 468 B.C., at the age of twenty-eight, Sophocles won his first victory as a playwright, defeating Aeschylus for the honors. At age eighty, he served on an interim government, following the debacle of the Athenian expedition to Syracuse in 413 B.C.

Sophocles' greatest surviving works are those of the Oedipus trilogy: *Oedipus the King*, *Oedipus at Colonus*, and *Antigone*. He

Sophocles.

is credited with introducing a third actor to the stage, enlarging the chorus from twelve to fifteen persons, and allowing the plays of a tetralogy to have separate themes so that they could stand on their own.

Euripides

Legend has it that the last of the great trio of tragic Athenian playwrights, Euripides (*c.* 480–406 B.C.), was born on the island of Salamis on the very day that Athens defeated the Persian fleet. It is also said that Euripides was extremely asocial, rejected the glitter of Athenian social life, and spent most of his life in a cave on Salamis. Though the sensitive depiction of his two greatest tragic heroines, Medea and Phaedra, certainly belie it, Euripides also had a widely current reputation as a misogynist.

What is known is that Euripides won only five first prizes at the Dionysia. The first of these was awarded in 442 B.C., eight years after his first play was performed; the last was given posthumously in 405 B.C. for *The Bacchae*. In 408 B.C., as democracy was crumbling in Athens, Euripides went into voluntary exile in Macedonia. He died there two years later.

Architecture and Sculpture

Among the fruits of victory over the Persians were the temples built to honor the Greeks' newly-exalted sense of their civilizations' worth, and that of its heroes, legends, myths, gods, and goddesses.

The dominant architectural and sculptural work of the first half of the fifth century B.C. was done at Olympia, where the building of the Temple of Zeus and its attendant sculptures and friezes took almost a generation. Finished in 456 B.C. to become one of the Seven Wonders of the World, the temple was built to honor a time and code of ethics then passing, when competition between the Greek city-states was acted out in the Olympic games rather than on the battlefield. As such, the Temple of Zeus marked the transition between the Archaic and Classical Ages.

In contrast, the next architectural masterpiece of the Greeks, the Parthenon in Athens, celebrates the triumph of civilization (i.e., Athens) over barbarism (i.e., the Persians and the Spartans) in the form of Amazons, Lapiths (centaurs), Trojans, and Giants. Begun nine years after the Temple of Zeus, the Parthenon is deliberately higher, wider, and longer than its predecessor; its centerpiece, an immense gold-and-ivory plated statue of Athena, is brighter than a similar one of the old Zeus at Olympia.

All of the notable sculptures of this period have lost the lightness and smiling regard of the Archaic Age. Just as the goat songs in honor of Dionysos developed into a theater of tragedies, so too had the sculptures come to reflect the deep seriousness of life. Among those that have survived from this period are the *Charioteer of Delphi* (476 B.C.), the great *Zeus* ready to throw his thunderbolt (c. 475 B.C.), and Myron's *The Discus Thrower* (c. 470 B.C.).

Philosophy in the Early Fifth Century B.C.

When Pythagoras died in southern Italy in 497 B.C., the mainstream of Greek philosophical development passed over to the Eleatic School in Sicily, at whose head was the great thinker, Parmenides. Although a mystic, he gave primary importance to reason and logic as the ultimate judges of reality.

A reconstruction of the great 40-foot statue of the goddess Athena in the Parthenon. Royal Ontario Museum, Toronto.

The goddess Athena mourning her dead Athenian soldiers (c. 460 B.C.).

In 475 B.C., Zeno of Elea succeeded Parmenides as head of the School and originated the dialectic form of argument that would be so famously employed by Socrates. Zeno also posed paradoxes such as proving that motion was inconceivable in a divisible reality, thereby further refining the original demonstration by Parmenides that Achilles could never catch the tortoise.

In 462 B.C., another refugee from Ionia arrived in Athens: the philosopher and failed landowner, Anaxagoras (c. 500-428 B.C.). The first philosopher in the city, he was welcomed as such by its society. The rising young Democrat, Pericles, subsidized Anaxagoras and became his pupil, as would Euripides and, most likely, Socrates.

In contrast to his predecessors' theories about the origin of the universe — that the basic substance was one of the four elements: earth, air, fire, or water — Anaxagoras postulated a universe made up of tiny, invisible particles all set in motion by a single, indivisible mind called the *nous* ("reason," "mind"). He also theorized that the sun was a mass of burning stone and that the phases of the moon were caused by the earth's shadow.

In Sicily, the philosopher Empedocles (c. 493–433 B.C.), the first of the Pluralists, declared that everything was composed of all of the basic elements. The opposing forces of Love and Hate, he further theorized, divided and recombined the elements into the infinite phenomena that our senses perceive.

At the same time, at Abdera on the Thracian coast, a radically different theory emerged. Leucippus, a philosopher and teacher of Democritus, postulated that the world is composed of tiny, indivisible particles called "atoms" (*a* = "not," *tome* = "separation," "cut"). Today, Leucippus is credited with being the father of atomic theory.

Herodotus

The great Greek historian Herodotus (*c.* 484–425 B.C.) left Athens in 443 B.C. to settle at the Athenian colony at Thurii (Italy). There, he spent the rest of his life finishing his "research" (*historia*) of the Persian Wars.

Herodotus was born on the Ionian coast at Halicarnassus (now Bodrum, Turkey). Exiled by the Persians in 457 B.C. for subversive activities, he traveled widely in Asia Minor, Babylonia, Egypt, and Greece — all the while gathering first-hand material for his book. In 447 B.C., he was attracted to Athens by its cultural flowering, and he came to be greatly admired by its leading intellects.

Herodotus' *History* was the first of its kind, not only as a creative work written in prose but also as a work of historical research. He is therefore known as the "father of history." Truly encyclopedic, his book deals with the history, legends, traditions, and customs of the ancient world as part of a course of events that leads inevitably to the great conflict between Greece and Athens. His basic point of view is that although men's lives are ruled by the blind chance of Fate, they are nevertheless responsible for the moral choices they make.

The Thirty Years' Peace

Essentially a cold war, this period was fraught with the knowledge that overt hostilities could erupt at any moment. Accordingly, it was characterized by constant jockeying between the city-states of the Peloponnesian League and those of the Athenian Empire to gain the edge when a conflict finally did break out.

In the meantime, Pericles forged ahead with his dream of Athens as a magnificent cultural center; he continued construction on the Acropolis and other projects, and infused artists and writers with his vision.

Pericles consolidated his power in 443 B.C., when the assembly voted for his democratic policies over those of the conservative opposition leader, Thucydides (not the historian). The defeated leader was then ostracized.

The following year, the Odeon ("music hall") was constructed on the side of the Acropolis and the Frieze of the Parthenon was begun (to be completed in 438 B.C.). Pericles was director of the festival, where Sophocles, just elected a general, presented *Antigone*.

In the sixth year of the Thirty Years' Peace (440 B.C.), war broke out between Samos and Miletus. When Athens was asked by Miletus to intervene, it took advantage of this request to set up a democracy in Samos. With the help of the Persians, the Samians and Byzantiums started an armed revolt; an Athenian fleet led by Pericles sailed to Samos to repress it. Although it took a savage nine months' siege, the revolt was successfully quelled and Athens was able to add both Samos and Byzantium to its empire.

In the same year, the temple of Poseidon at Sounion was completed. The great Athenian sculptor, Pheidias, finished his giant statue of Athena Parthenon ("Virgin") in 438 B.C. and had it dedicated in the building of that name. At the Dionysia, Euripides' *Alcestis* was performed. In 437 B.C., work began on the Propylaea ("portals") of the Acropolis.

The Acropolis in Athens.

Athens continued to expand its empire with the foundation of Amphipolis, a rich (and, to the Spartans, disturbing) source of ship-building timber, on the Macedonian coast.

In 435–434 B.C., war broke out between Spartan-allied Corinth and independent Korcyra (Corfu). Korcyra asked Athens for aid and, because of Korcyra's strategic importance and the considered inevitability of war with the Peloponnesian League, Athens agreed to a defensive alliance in 433 B.C. In breach of its peace treaty with Sparta, Athens then fought Corinth to save Korcyra from defeat at sea.

Athens subsequently ordered Potidaea, a former Corinthian colony in Macedonia that had since become a part of the Athenian alliance, to raze its seawalls and expel the remaining Corinthians. Potidaea refused, having received guarantees of aid from Sparta. Athens began besieging the city. During one of the battles, Socrates saved the life of an orphaned Alcibiades, who would later become his disciple.

In Athens, resentment of Pericles' power resulted in attacks on his closest associates: the sculptor Pheidias, the philosopher Anaxagoras, and the famous courtesan (*hetaera*) Aspasia, who was Pericles' mistress and mother of his son (also named Pericles). They were all brought to trial around 432 B.C. on differing charges of impiety.

Pheidias was imprisoned, where he died, perhaps from poison; Anaxagoras went into exile to escape being forced to take hemlock; and Aspasia was acquitted, but only after Pericles tearfully begged for mercy before a court of fifteen hundred jurors. This emotive display led Plutarch and others to suspect that Pericles was guilty of the charges and that he had provoked the conflict with Sparta in order to divert attention from himself. But by this time, the plunge into full-scale war had acquired its own momentum.

In 431 B.C., Sparta called a conference of the Peloponnesian League, where it heard complaints from Megara and Aegina, among others, that Athens had violated the peace treaty. The Athenian delegate to Sparta dismissed the charges in an insulting and provocative speech. Fearful of a further expansion of Athenian power, however, Sparta reluctantly accepted its allies' complaints and judged that the treaty had been broken and that war must be declared. After assurances from the oracle at Delphi that they would be victorious, the Spartans demanded that Athens lift the siege of Potidaea, respect the independence of Aegina, and revoke a decree prohibiting Megara's use of Athenian harbors.

Bolstered by Pericles' assurances that the Spartans would never be able to match Athenian sea power, the city's assembly rejected Sparta's demands. War thus became inevitable.

The Second Peloponnesian War

The war began in 431 B.C. as the Spartan king, Archidamos, invaded Attica. (Thus, this beginning phase is called the Archidamanian War.) Pericles, counting on his navy to win, refused to engage the Spartans in land battles and instead had the Athenians withdraw behind the Long Walls of Piraeus and Athens. His plan was to feed the city via a supply line of ships to the rest of the empire, particularly the Black Sea area, and to leave the

Spartans to wear themselves out. The latter did just that, ravaging the countryside to no avail, with neither battles nor victories to sustain morale.

Athens sent its fleet out to raid the Peloponnese and forced Archidamos to return to Sparta. The fleet also attacked other areas of the Spartan alliance; in the summer of 431 B.C., Pericles led an army to ravage nearby Megara.

In the winter of that year, Pericles delivered his famous Funeral Oration for the fallen Athens. The speech (quoted in Thucydides' history of the Peloponnesian War) describes the development of the democracy for which the Athenian soldiers gave their lives and applauds the glory of its fruits.

That same year, Euripides' *Medea* was produced at the Dionysia.

A plague (probably yellow fever) broke out within the walls of densely-populated Athens the following summer. The renowned physician, Hippocrates of Cos, was summoned to aid the city; however, the disease ultimately killed roughly one-third of Athens' population.

Though Pericles' two legitimate sons died from the plague, the assembly held him responsible for the catastrophe, tried him for misusing public funds, fined him, and removed him from power.

In the same year, Phideas' statue of Zeus was installed at Spartan-controlled Olympia; at Athens, Euripides' *Hippolytus* was produced.

Popular demand resulted in Pericles' reinstatement in 429 B.C, by which time he was deathly ill with the plague. In a fit of remorse, the assembly granted citizenship to his illegitimate son by the Miletus-born Aspasia.

That summer, two and a half years after the recommencement of the Peloponnesian Wars, Pericles died. And, according to Thucydides, all hopes of an Athenian victory died with him.

Theater, Philosophy, and History in the Late Classical Age

Among the most remarkable accomplishments of this age was the cultural and intellectual development in Athenian-controlled territory, which continued unabated in the face of war and plague, and the tenuous atmosphere that such harsh conditions inevitably breed.

In the third year of the war, the Dionysia still conducted its annual drama festivals, and philosophical inquiry was in full and sometimes irreverent swing.

Aristophanes

Athenian-born and an arch-conservative favoring aristocratic rule, Aristophanes, the greatest of comic playwrights (448–385 B.C.), produced his first three satires — one of which, *The Acharnians*, advocated ending the war with Sparta — under a pseudonym. Classified as "Old Comedy," his plays are a mixture of burlesque, puns, parody, farce, and satire. They have as their targets the new politicians (particularly Pericles' successor, Cleon); playwrights such as Euripides; and philosophers, specifically the Sophists and Socrates. Of the more than forty plays Aristophanes wrote, only eleven have survived. The most famous and enduring of these is the satire, *Lysistrata*, in which Athenian women attempt to end a war by withholding sexual favors from men.

Democritus

In Athenian-allied Abdera on the coast of Thrace, the philosopher Democritus (*c.* 460–370 B.C.) developed and refined the atomic theory of Leucippus. Democritus is known as the "Laughing Philosopher" because of his belief that cheerfulness — developed through moderation, calm, and freedom from fear — is the highest good. His atomic theory put an end to rampant philosophical speculations about the nature of the universe and created the basis of modern science.

The Sophists

In reaction to seemingly pointless cosmological theorizing, a group of philosophers known as Sophists ("wise ones") began to teach practical philosophy such as rhetoric, and for this wisdom they charged a practical fee. The most famous of these philosophers was Protagoras of Abdera (*c.* 480–411 B.C.), who traveled to Sicily and Magna Graecia before arriving in Athens. He originated the subjective philosophical stance that "man is the measure of all things." The Sophist Georgias of Leotini, who arrived in Athens in 427 B.C. as a diplomat and stayed to teach rhetoric, similarly argued that there is nothing that reason can know beyond what the senses can communicate.

Socrates

Born in Athens to a sculptor and a midwife, Socrates (*c.* 470–
399 B.C.) fought with distinction as an infantryman in the battles
of Potidaea, Delium (424 B.C.), and Amphipolis (422 B.C.). After
serving in the army, he pursued a radically different career: an
engagement in philosophical discourse and enquiry in the mar-
ketplaces and other public venues. Specifically, Socrates sought
a basis for ethical behavior in the knowledge of such concepts as
love, truth, justice, and above all, in the knowledge of one's self.
Though he didn't write books, his investigations were recorded
by a then young wrestler named Plato. Another of Socrates'
pupils, Alcibiades, became a leading Athenian general, but was
toppled by pride and the paranoid conservative backlash that
would eventually cause Socrates himself to be condemned to
death in 399 B.C.

Thucydides

Born of an aristocratic family with ties in Athens and Thrace,
Thucydides (*c.* 460– 400 B.C.) may have been related to both Miltiades, the hero of Marathon, and Kimon, the commander of the
battle of Salamis. When war broke out with Sparta, Thucydides
was aware of its long-term importance and immediately began
preparations to write its history. Surviving the plague, he was
elected general in 424 B.C. and sent to Thasos off the Thracian
coast. From there, under General Brasidas, Thucydides com-
manded a fleet ordered to stop the Spartans from taking timber-
rich Amphipolis. After the failure of this expedition, Thucydides

Socrates.

was exiled to Thrace, where he spent the next twenty years writing the extraordinary and fascinating *History of the Peloponnesian War*. This work, as he himself explained, is buttressed by eyewitness accounts and recollections of the era's major speeches — which, if not recorded verbatim, are at least reported in their true spirit. Thucydides' account was left incomplete, however, abruptly ending in 411 B.C. Soon after the general amnesty declared at the end of the war in 404 B.C., Thucydides returned to Athens, where he died.

The War Continues

After the death of Pericles and the subsidence of the plague, Athens showed no signs of capitulation.

The Athenians took Potidea in 429 B.C.; the Spartans, in turn, besieged and forced the surrender of the Athenian ally, Plataia.

In 428–427 B.C., Athenian forces suppressed a revolt on the northern Aegean island of Mytilene (Lesbos). In the subsequent assembly debate on what kind of punishment to mete out, the Athenian general Cleon recommended that the entire male population of Mytilene be put to death. The order was later rescinded, but not before the execution of approximately one thousand Mytilenean men. Meanwhile, battles between the Athenian fleet and the Spartans continued to take place around the Peloponnese.

In 425 B.C., the Spartans landed on the island of Sphacteria, off the western coast of the Peloponnesian, and blockaded the fort that the Athenians had established at Pylos. Cleon, whose hard-line policies had established him as the first demagogue, was challenged in the Athenian Assembly; his reputation at stake, the general went to Pylos and relieved the blockade, forcing the unprecedented surrender of Spartan troops in the process. When Sparta then sued for peace, it was Cleon, now the unquestioned leader of the Assembly, who rejected the offer. This refusal prompted Aristophanes to write *The Acharnians*.

The brilliant Spartan general, Brasidas, took over conduct of the war for the Peloponnesian League in 424 B.C. Athens was defeated at Delium by the Boetians — a battle in which Socrates distinguished himself by being the last man to retreat.

Brasidas took Amphipolis in 422 B.C., thereby causing the disgrace and exile of Thucydides, who then retired to finish his history. In a later battle at Amphipolis, Brasidas was wounded and died shortly after hearing of the Spartan victory. While trying to retreat, Cleon was also killed.

Cleon's death assured the ascendancy of Nicias, the leader of the oligarchy party, to leadership in Athens; the young Alcibiades headed the opposition Democrats.

Without the presence of the two principal opponents of a settlement, Brasidas and Cleon, the "Peace of Nicias" was negotiated between Athens and Sparta in 422 B.C. This fifty-year pact seemed to end the war, which had raged on for ten years.

Thucydides, however, made the point that the agreement did not herald a genuine peace, but rather a lull in what would be a much longer conflict.

Problems erupted almost immediately after the pact was signed, when a peace treaty between Argos and Sparta expired.

With fear now spreading among the smaller city-states that an alliance between Sparta and Athens would mean a joint attempt to dominate the country, Corinth counseled Argos not to trust the Spartans and to make allies with other city-states. This stratagem was symptomatic of the considerable jockeying that occurred among smaller powers to maintain some sort of independence amidst rampant distrust.

In 420 B.C., after maneuvers by Alcibiades, the Athenian Assembly finally agreed to an alliance with Argo and their allies, the Peloponnesian cities of Elis and Mantinea. With this alliance, war between Athens and Sparta resumed, although neither city-state officially renounced the "Peace of Nicias."

Just recently elected general in his first year of eligibility, Alcibiades led a small expeditionary force into the Peloponnese during the summer of 419 B.C. Picking up allies along the way, he shattered the last vestiges of peace with Sparta.

One year later, the Spartans attacked Argos and defeated the allied forces of Athens and Argos at the battle of Mantinea. With an anti-democratic regime now installed in Argos, the city-state signed a thirty-year peace treaty with Sparta. A democratic faction quickly overthrew the pro-Spartan oligarchs, however, and immediately re-established an alliance with Athens.

The Athenians then sent a force to subdue the Spartan colony on the island of Melos, whose residents counterattacked in 416 B.C. to no avail. Though the Melians surrendered, the men were subsequently executed and the women and children enslaved. Satisfied that a lesson had been learned by other city-states, Athens then re-colonized Melos with its own citizens.

The Sicilian Expedition

In 415 B.C., the Sicilian city of Segesta requested Athenian military aid against the neighboring city-state of Selinous. Alcibiades, again elected general, viewed this as an opportunity to expand Athenian presence to the west of the Peloponnese. At his urging, the Athenian Assembly sent a fleet to conquer the entire island and prevent rumored plans by Syracuse to establish hegemony over Sicily.

But just prior to the fleet's departure, someone — perhaps in a plot to discredit Alcibiades and the democratic faction — disfigured nearly all the busts of Hermes in Athens. As it jeopardized the success of the impending expedition, this serious act of impiety could not be left unpunished. Alcibiades was immediately accused of the crime — a consequence, no doubt, of his carousing and general lack of respect for usual proprieties. He demanded a trial but was instead ordered to sail to Sicily with his army while the investigation continued.

No sooner had his ships arrived in Sicily, than Alcibiades was ordered to return to Athens (without his soldiers) and stand trial. He jumped ship in southern Italy and fled to Sparta. Put on trial *in abstensia* by the Athenian Assembly, Alcibiades was convicted and condemned to death.

Nicias, now commander of the Athenian army, besieged Syracuse in 414 B.C. The Spartans reacted, at Alcibiades' urging, by dispatching "volunteer" forces to aid Syracuse. This Spartan-led army turned the tide of the battle, and the Athenians quickly found themselves besieged with their backs to the harbor.

Athens sent a large fleet of reinforcements under General Demosthenes, but his indecisive leadership and an unpropitious eclipse of the moon resulted in the demoralization and eventual slaughter of the Athenian force. The fleet was entirely destroyed; Nicias and Demosthenes were executed; and the surviving seven thousand Athenians were sent to the quarries of Syracuse to die of exposure and malnutrition.

Again heeding Alcibiades' advice, Sparta established a fortress at Decelea that cut off Athens' food supply from Euboea and its silver supply from Lauriam — both vital elements to the city's resistance from behind its own walls.

Sensing an Athenian defeat, various members of the Delian League defected in 412 B.C. Among these were Byzantion, a commanding strategic point on the Bosphorus, and Thasos, which controlled gold and timber supplies on the Thracian coast.

In return for guaranteed hegemony over Ionian cities, Persia entered the war as a Spartan ally. The resulting influx of Persian gold and men decisively and irrecoverably tipped the balance of power to the side of the Spartans.

At this extremely critical moment, facing defeat, the Athenian Assembly voted to exempt poets from military service abroad.

The following year (411 B.C.), a council of four hundred oligarchs seized power in Athens and tried to make peace on reasonable terms with Sparta. They were unsuccessful, however, as the Athenian army and the fleet at Samos refused to join their coup. Moderate Athenian aristocrats staged a countercoup four months later, and set up the Council of 5,000 to rule Athens. When this government collapsed, the Democratic constitution was restored in 410 B.C. Alcibiades was recalled as a general

Demosthenes.

and joined the Athenian fleet at Samos, after having fled Sparta for Ionia because of a dangerous liaison with the Spartan king's wife.

Instead of returning to Athens as expected, Alcibiades sailed north and smashed the Spartan fleet as it was trying to gain control of the Hellespont. He then began the two-year task of restoring Athenian control over food-supply lines from the Black Sea.

In 408 B.C., the 79-year-old Euripides was cleared of a prior indictment for impiety, but chose to go into voluntary exile at the invitation of the Macedonian King Archelaus. Before Euripides' departure, *Orestes* was produced at the Athenian Dionysia.

Alcibiades triumphantly returned to Athens in 407 B.C., before leaving to rejoin his fleet off the Ionian coast. In the meantime, however, Lysander's Spartan force had routed the Athenian fleet at the battle of Notium (near Ephesus). Once again, the Athenian Assembly censured Alcibiades and removed him from office. He fled for refuge — this time to a private castle on the Hellespont.

The Athenian navy defeated the Spartans at the battle of Arginusae near Mytilene in 406 B.C.; but, in an ensuing storm, twenty-five Athenian ships were sunk and their crews drowned. The Athenian Assembly, anxious to place blame, condemned the naval generals to death — among them, the son of Pericles and Aspasia. Socrates, a member of the presiding committee that day, dissented but was outvoted. However, once the generals were executed, the assembly quickly repented and condemned to death those who had recommended the executions.

At about this time, Sparta attempted to reach a peace settlement but was rejected.

The year 406 B.C. also saw the deaths of 90-year-old Sophocles in Athens and Euripides in Macedonia, where the latter had written *The Bacchae* and *Iphigenia in Aulis*.

The Athenians sailed north to engage the Spartans in the Hellespont in 405 B.C, anchoring at the strategically vulnerable area of Aegospotami. Alcibiades could see them from his castle and rode down to advise his countrymen against taking a position without a posterior food-supplying harbor. His help was rejected, however, and he returned to the castle.

Lysander's Spartans attacked the harboring Athenian ships, destroyed nearly the entire fleet, and executed four thousand captives. The Spartans were then masters of the Aegean and, thus, of Athenian food supplies.

Lysander moved to eliminate Alcibiades, having him assassinated on orders from the Persian king. Afterwards, Lysander set sail to besiege Athens.

Its food supply exhausted and its streets full of the dead and dying, Athens capitulated unconditionally the following year. Though Lysander demanded that the Long Walls be leveled and that the oligarchs return from exile, he left Athens some of its shattered dignity by not enslaving the entire population. Also against custom, he allowed the city to retain twelve warships on the guarantee that they would be pledged in allegiance to future Spartan causes. The returning oligarchs, headed by Kritias, were established as the infamous Council of Thirty, which instituted a reactionary reign of terror against democratic, anti-Spartan elements in Athens. At the same time, Thucydides was allowed to return from exile, while Socrates was banned from public discourses.

A year later, the "Thirty Tyrants" (as they were then called) were overthrown by rebel democratic forces led by Thrasybolus. With Kritias already dead, Lysander moved to crush the revolt, but was overruled by Pausanias, the Spartan king. Democracy was restored in Athens.

Nevertheless, it was a democracy that was forced to look uncomfortably over its shoulder at the Spartans and carefully avoid provoking their re-intervention. At the same time, there were a lot of old scores to be settled.

Several of these involved resentments against the self-professed gadfly, Socrates. In 399 B.C., at the age of seventy, he was accused and convicted of attempting to introduce new gods (*daimonion*) and of corrupting the young. The intent seems to have been to force him into exile; but Socrates adamantly refused to forsake his principles, or to accept banishment or a pre-arranged escape from jail. Therefore, he was reluctantly condemned to death by drinking hemlock. All of his friends and pupils, except the ill Plato, were present as Socrates died in his cell.

Thucydides also died that year, bringing the fifth century and the Golden Age of Classical Greece to an end.

CLASSICAL GREECE:
THE FOURTH CENTURY B.C.

This first half of the fourth century was marked by struggles for dominance between Sparta, Athens, and the newly emergent Thebes — with Cyrus II's Persia free to make alliances and thus holding the balance of power. The second half was marked by the sudden rise of Macedonia under Philip II and his son, Alexander.

Athens continued to be Greece's cultural center, although at a considerably diminished pace, particularly during the century's first half. In the late fourth century, one of Greece's greatest sculptors, Praxiteles, flourished; on stage, the Athenian playwright Menander promulgated the "New Comedy"; and the soldier-historian Xenophon continued the grand tradition of Herodotus and Thucydides.

In philosophy, it was an era first of Plato, then of the Cynics, and finally of Aristotle, the latter ending his years and the century as the highly influential tutor of Alexander the Great.

Plato

Plato (428-347 B.C.) was born to an aristocratic family whose lineage was said to include Solon and the early kings of Athens. He first gained fame as a wrestler and then nurtured political ambitions. After being disillusioned by the actions of the assembly during the war, however, he became a pupil of Socrates.

Philip II of Macedonia, father of Alexander the Great.

Plato.

Following Socrates' death, Plato took refuge with the philosopher Euclid at Megara. He then traveled to Italy and Sicily and possibly Egypt, all the while writing his Socratic dialogues. Permanently returning to Athens sometime before 387 B.C., he founded an Academy there. The Academy has been called the first European university, with a curriculum that focused not only on philosophy, but also on biology, mathematics, astronomy, and political theory.

After teaching and writing for twenty years, Plato returned to Sicily in 367 B.C. and attempted to put into practice the philosophical and political theories he had been developing in his books, particularly *The Republic*. There, he tutored Syracuse's new ruler, Dionysos the Younger. While Plato was thus engaged, the young Aristotle traveled to Athens from Macedonia and enrolled in the Academy.

Making two more trips to Syracuse, Plato became increasingly disillusioned with its ruler and returned to Athens, devoting himself to writing his final works. He died in Athens in 347 B.C. but his Academy would remain open for another seven hundred years, until it was closed by the Byzantine emperor, Justinian, for its unacceptable "pagan" teachings.

Aristotle

Aristotle (384–321 B.C.) was born in Stagira, a Greek colony in Chalkidiki on the Thracian Sea. His mother was from a prominent family in Euboea, while his father was court physician to King Amyntas II of Macedonia. From his mother, Aristotle inherited an ambivalence about his "country" background in Macedonia;

Aristotle.

from his father, he gained a deep interest in the sciences and their empirical approach to knowledge.

At the age of seventeen, Aristotle enrolled in Plato's Academy, where he rounded off his education in the areas of ethics, aesthetics, and general philosophy. But he was never much of a Platonist, preferring reality–based scientific methods to the more mystical bent of Plato's Forms.

After Plato's death in 347 B.C., Aristotle left Athens and eventually became attached to the court of an old friend, Hermias. After Hermias was captured and executed by the Persians, Aristotle accepted a job tutoring the teen-age Alexander at Pella, the Macedonian palace. Aristotle stayed there until Alexander became king, at which point the philosopher returned to Athens and opened a school, the Lyceum. Its graduates became known as the "Peripatetic School," due to the walks or strolls (*peripetia*) they took around the grounds while discussing philosophical matters.

Of the approximately four hundred works that Aristotle wrote, only fifty have survived. Among the greatest contributions in his encyclopedic treatment of the world are the *Nichomachaean Ethics*, the *Poetics*, and his emphasis on deductive, analytical, and empirical logic rather than Platonic dialectical reasoning.

Following Alexander's death and the consequent anti-Macedonian atmosphere in Athens, Aristotle moved to a family estate in Euboea, where he died a year later.

Xenophon

Born to a land-owning family near Athens, Xenophon (*c.* 430–355 B.C.) was a follower of Socrates before he joined a group of

Greek mercenaries in a campaign by the Persian prince Cyrus the Younger to unseat his brother. After Cyrus was killed and the Greeks' officers treacherously murdered, Xenophon was chosen to lead the ten thousand surviving mercenaries on a 1,500-mile march to safety. He later chronicled this journey in his most famous work, the *Anabasis* ("Military Expedition"). As he was not allowed to return to Athens due to his Persian service, he joined the Spartans in expeditions against Persian despots in Ionia and against Thebes and their Athenian allies. The Spartan king awarded Xenophon a country estate near Olympia, while Athens branded him a traitor and banished him for life. But when Athens and Sparta later became allies against Thebes, the ban against Xenophon was lifted.

The most important of Xenophon's other thirteen works are *Cyropaedia*, a hagiography of Cyrus the Great, and the *Hellenica*, which chronicles Greek history from 411 B.C. (where Thucydides ended) to 363 B.C. His works on Socrates are considered far inferior to those of Plato.

After sending two of his sons to fight in the Athenian cavalry (where one died), he spent his remaining years not in Athens, but in Corinth.

The Battle for Hegemony in Greece: 399–346 B.C.

As chronicled in Xenophon's *Hellenica*, the years between the death of Socrates in 399 B.C. and that of Plato in 347 B.C. were marked by power struggles — struggles between the region's great city-states, including the newly ascendant Thebes and Macedonia, to gain hegemony in Greece.

After Persia retaliated against the Ionian cities that had taken part in Cyrus' *Anabasis*, Sparta came to their aid in 399 B.C.; the ensuing four-year campaign proved Greece's continuing superiority over Persian forces. In retaliation, Persia fomented unrest in Corinth and encouraged it to form an alliance with Athens, Thebes, and Argos against Sparta. After several battles (one of which claimed the Spartan general, Lysander), an allied fleet under the command of the Athenian general, Konon, soundly defeated the Spartans at the battle of Knidos in 394 B.C. Sparta withdrew its army back into the Peloponnese, temporarily leaving the field to the allies.

As a result, Athens rebuilt its Long Walls (ironically, with Persian aid), and turned its attention to re-establishing its empire. But soon, Sparta was back in the field. After a series of battles in 386 B.C., the Spartans and the Persians came to terms on a Persian-imposed "King's Peace." This settlement left Ionia in Persian hands, allowed Athens to retain certain islands, and freed the other Greek city-states from all alliances; it did not effect the treaties binding the Peloponnesian League together, however, and Sparta soon re-imposed its will on various parts of the Greek mainland.

In 382–379 B.C., Sparta executed two actions that would have far-reaching consequences: it demolished the power of the northern city-state of Olynthos in an attempt to gain hegemony in Macedonia; and it aided an oligarchic coup in Thebes, after which it established a garrison in the city.

The campaign against Olynthos created a power vacuum that would eventually allow Macedonia's hegemony over Greece. More immediately, the aid provided to the oligarchs in Thebes gave rise to a war that would destroy Sparta's power and leave Thebes the dominant state in Greece — for the time being.

The resentment and paranoia generated by Sparta's garrison in Thebes first manifested itself in a counter-coup in 379 B.C.: seven exiles, disguised as women, snuck back into the city at night and knifed Spartan sympathizers. The exiles then freed one hundred and fifty compatriots and roused the rest of the city so greatly that the Spartans were forced to flee.

Athens allied itself with Thebes in the war that followed, forming, in the process, an Athenian Naval Confederacy similar to the previous century's Delian League. Thebes soon became the dominant power in Greece by crushing the Spartans at the battle of Leuktra in 371 B.C.

But when Thebes invaded the Peloponnese the following year, Athens, fearing Theban dominance, sided with Sparta for the first time since the wars with the Persians. At the battle of Mantinea in 362 B.C. — the Thebans' fourth attempt to invade the Peloponnese — they were finally victorious over the Spartan-Athenian alliance. With Thebes' leading general lost and all sides exhausted, however, the Greek states agreed to peace. It is at this point that Xenophon's history of Greece concludes.

Three years later (359 B.C.), after the death of King Perdiccas in a battle with the Illyrians, Philip II succeeded his father on the Macedonian throne.

The Macedonians

The Macedonians had been accepted as Greek since at least 459 B.C., when their king, Alexander I, was invited to compete in the strictly Greek Olympics. However, the Greek that the Macedonians spoke was rough and "barbarian" (a Greek word originally equivalent to "gobbledygook" in English); their kingdom was such a piecemeal scattering of forts that they were virtually discounted by Athens and Sparta as a serious political entity.

Philip II changed this perception. Taking the throne at age twenty-two, he almost immediately proved himself to be a genius of both military tactics and diplomacy. A year later, he invaded Thrace and claimed Amphipolis and the nearby gold mines of the Pangeon Mountains; at the same time, he founded Philippi to control access to them from the east. Athens, although embroiled in a "Social War" to suppress the revolt of several confederacy members, declared war on Philip in 357 B.C.

The following year, Philip captured Potidea and its Athenian garrison and released the latter unharmed. By handing the city back to its natives, he earned their solid allegiance against the Athenians. With this victory came the news that he had a son, Alexander, born to him and his Ephesian wife, Olympias. On this most propitious day, Philip also learned that his horse had triumphed in the Olympics, and that his general Parmenion had been victorious against the Illyrians.

Additionally, this was said to be the day when fire destroyed the great temple of Artemis at Ephesus, while the goddess herself was away attending Alexander's birth. The destruction of her temple was considered a harbinger of disaster for the people of Asia.

Over the next eighteen years, Philip consolidated his power in the north by razing Olynthos, taking control of the shrine at Delphi, and forging an alliance with Thebes. In 369 B.C., he summoned Aristotle from the Athenian Academy to tutor the 13-year-old Alexander in Macedonia.

Throughout this period, Philip was vilified by the Athenian orator and demagogue, Demosthenes, who eventually convinced his reluctant compatriots to wage further war against Macedonia.

At the battle of Chaeronea in Boiotia in 338 B.C., Philip defeated the allied forces of Athens and Thebes, thereby establishing Macedonian hegemony over Greece, with the exception of Sparta. A year later, he created the Corinthian League of Greek city-states and declared war on Persia, after sending Parmenion there to secure a beachhead.

But the polygamous Philip never made it to Asia. He was assassinated at his daughter's wedding party in the theater at Aigai (Vergina) in 336 B.C. As a son had recently been born to Philip and his new and favored Macedonian wife — a son who may have eventually usurped Alexander's successorship — some speculate that a fearful Olympias instigated the assassination. What is known is that the infant pretender was killed almost immediately after his father's assassination; furthermore, it was not until after the death of Olympias' other enemies, that the Macedonian barony confirmed Alexander's accession.

Alexander imposed his will upon Philip's empire and prepared to invade Persia — an act, he told the Greeks, meant to avenge the sacrileges perpetrated on Greek shrines during the Persian invasion of 480 B.C. He was twenty years old.

THE AGE OF ALEXANDER

Alexander literally took the world by storm. A year after succeeding his father, he consolidated Macedonia's northern borders and leveled Thebes for having presumed to revolt against his authority. A year after that, while leaving Philip's general Antipater in charge of Greece, Alexander crossed the Bosphorus into Asia with an invasion force of Greeks and Macedonians.

Alexander made a pilgrimage to the ruins of Troy in order to pay homage at the grave of Achilles, to whom Aristotle had introduced him in their study of *The Iliad*. Carrying Achilles' shield into battle, as legend would have it, Alexander routed a Persian force at the Granicus River. Within a year, he had conquered Asia Minor and liberated the cities of Ionia.

After establishing the one-eyed Antigonus as satrap of Phrygia, Alexander went to meet his reinforcements at Gordium in 333 B.C. Failing to undo the city's famous Gordian knot of cornel bark, he impatiently sliced through it with his sword and departed in search of Darius III, the Persian king. Five months later, he found Darius and the Persian army of some 100,000 to 200,000 soldiers at Issus on the Syrian-Cilician border. Alexander's forces shattered those of Darius, who was nearly captured during the single great battle.

In 332 B.C., Alexander captured Tyre and Jerusalem, founded Alexandria, and visited the oracle of the ram-headed god Ammon at Siwah in the Egyptian-Libyan desert.

In Greece, Antipater put down a Spartan uprising in 331 B.C.; meanwhile, at Gaugamela in Mesopotamia, Alexander defeated

Alexander the Great.

Alexander the Great depicted as the son of the god Zeus Ammon. Thracian coin (3ʳᵈ century B.C.).

another mammoth Persian army. Narrowly avoiding capture once more, Darius ignominiously fled into the Eurdish Mountains.

Proclaimed King of Asia, Alexander entered the wealthy cities of Babylon, Suza, Pasargadae, and Persepolis. He and his troops burned the latter city's great palace in 330 B.C. During this time, Darius was arrested by his followers and murdered by Bessus.

Alexander sent Darius' body back to Persepolis for royal burial, had himself declared legal inheritor of the throne, and began wearing Persian court dress. This self-elevation above his officers and troops caused considerable tension; within a year, the son of Parmenion, Philotas, was executed for failing to report a plot against Alexander. Alexander had Parmenion himself murdered to prevent retaliation.

Alexander extended his empire east into Bactria, where Bessus was captured and executed.

After campaigning against the Sogdians in 327 B.C., Alexander killed his general Cleitus in a drunken argument and married the most beautiful lady in Asia: Roxanne. He then attempted to impose the Persian custom of *proskynesis* (prostration before a royal personage) on his Macedonian officers.

There followed an assassination plot by Kallisthenes, Alexander's official historian and the nephew of Aristotle. When Kallisthenes was caught, Alexander had him executed.

Alexander then entered India. It was during this campaign that the philosophers Anaxarchus of Adbera and Pyrrho met the Brahmin Calanus and other gurus — each naked and thus dubbed the Gymnosophists or "Naked Philosophers." Their asceticism would have a deep influence on the course of Greek philosophy, particularly among the Stoics.

Alexander crossed the Indus River in 326 B.C. and defeated the Indian king, Porus, and his elephants in the battle of Hydapses. Alexander's famous horse, Bucephalus, who had given him twenty years of service, was fatally wounded during the battle.

Alexander pressed forward and conquered the Punjab; but his soldiers, some over sixty years old, refused to go any further. Alexander and his army therefore turned back, not knowing that the southern tip of India was only three months' march away.

Alexander and the army, accompanied by the 79-year-old Indian guru, Calanus, sailed down the Indus River to the Arabian Sea in the hopes of charting a new passage back to the Mediterranean. At a battle to take the fortress of Multan, Alexander was severely wounded in the lung and almost killed.

Upon reaching the Arabian Sea in 325 B.C., Alexander led a support group across the deadly Baluchistan desert, while his general, Nearchus, continued to sail along the coast. Each group nearly perished from hunger, thirst, and exposure before reaching Persepolis and the mouths of the Tigris and Euphrates rivers, respectively.

Nearchus rejoined Alexander and his forces at Susa in 324 B.C. Here, Calanus announced that the time had come for him to die. After telling Alexander that he would see him "at Babylon," Calanus had himself burnt alive on a funeral pyre. At the proceeding funeral games and festival, forty-two Indians died of alcohol poisoning.

Alexander arranged a mass wedding for his high-ranking Macedonian soldiers with more than ninety upper-class Iranian ladies, thus further implementing his policy of East-West integration. Always the fearless leader, he himself took two brides:

Alexander on his horse Bucephalus. Part of a mosaic from Pompeii showing the battle of Issus against Darius.

the daughters of Darius and of the previous king, Artaxerexes III. His general and possible lover, Hephaistion, married another daughter of Darius so that his children could be Alexander's nieces and nephews. Also wedded were some ten thousand Asian mistresses and common soldiers, who received an Alexandrian dowry to do so.

As a prelude to announcing that its veterans were to be sent home, Alexander paid off the army's accumulated debts. But the arrival of thirty thousand young Iranian replacements in the camp caused a near mutiny. Alexander bluffed his way through the insurrection, convincing the veterans, led by Kraterus, to return home and "watch over Greece." Alexander further assured them that the general Antipater would come east with fresh Macedonian troops.

Alexander and his troops headed towards Babylon via Hammadan, where Hephaistion became ill with fever, possibly typhoid. After lingering for eight days, the general died, and Alexander's grief was monumental. Two weeks passed before he was able to order the Lion of Hammadan (still there) to be carved as a memorial. He and his entourage then left for winter quarters in Babylon.

The winter of 323 B.C. was rife with portents and tales of Alexander's heavy drinking and dressing up as gods and goddesses at dinner parties. Alexander planned a conquest of Carthage and the rest of the Mediterranean shores around Spain to Sicily.

On May 29, Alexander became ill at a late-night drinking party and retired to his room. His condition progressively worsened over eleven days, until he was unable even to speak; but he was able to watch as his entire army filed by to personally see that he was still alive. Shortly afterwards, however, he died.

Most scholars agree that it was the fever that finally killed Alexander. Yet his death has also been attributed to heavy drinking in the wake of Hephaistion's death, as well as to a Macedonian conspiracy led by the son of Antipater, Cassander, who had recently joined him at Babylon.

Whatever the cause, Alexander was all of thirty-two when he died.

THE HELLENISTIC AGE

The Hellenistic period was one in which Alexander 's successors (*Diadochi*) sought to preserve his legacy, even as they established their own discrete zones of power. Ideally, these areas were to be impervious from take-over by the others, and to serve as possible bases from which to try for hegemony over the rest of the empire. In other words, while attempting to disseminate and enshrine Hellenism as a way of life superior to that of their "barbarian" subjects, the successors were simultaneously dividing it into divergent political pieces.

There were five *Diadochi*: Ptolemy in Egypt, Seleucus in Babylonia, Antigonus the One-Eyed in Asia Minor, Lysimachus in Thrace, and Antipater in Greece. Other prominent figures were Alexander's beautiful and pregnant wife, Roxanne; his feeble-minded half-brother, Arridaeus, who was the ostensible king of the empire (Philip III) under the regency of Perdiccas; and Alexander's mother, Olympias, who eventually poisoned Arridaeus in her attempt to consolidate power in Macedonia.

The Wars of the *Diadochi* were fought across the empire from 323 to 280 B.C., as the successors refused to accept the legitimacy first of Perdiccas' regency, and then of Alexander's son by Roxanne. During these struggles, Ptolemy gained possession of Alexander's embalmed body and put it on permanent display at Alexandria. It would later disappear during the riots at the end of the third century A.D.

In Greece, Antipater and Kraterus put down a revolt of the Greek city-states in the Lamian War in Thessaly of 323 B.C.

Suspected of complicity in Alexander's death and in danger because of his Macedonian ties and Demosthenes' demagoguery, Aristotle refused to "give Athenians a second chance to sin against philosophy." He instead fled Athens, as Socrates had not, and took refuge on his mother's estate in Chalkis (Euboea); the Athenians nevertheless sentenced him to death *in abstensia*. That same year, Roxanne gave birth to Alexander's son, Alexander IV.

Demosthenes, cornered by Macedonian soldiers in a sanctuary on the island of Poros, poisoned himself in 322 B.C. Aristotle died a short time later of a stomach ailment (or, say some, self-administered poison) in Euboean exile.

A year later in Egypt, Perdiccas was killed by his own troops, who were incited to mutiny by Ptolemy's propaganda. In a tripartite alliance, Cassander and Antigonus the One-Eyed were appointed royal generals and Antipater was named regent. The latter died of old age in 319 B.C.

Olympias murdered the half-wit co-ruler, Arridaeus, in a power struggle with Cassander in 317 B.C. However, her army besieged by Cassander's forces at Pydna, Olympias surrendered the following year and was swiftly executed. Cassander established a new city on the Thermaic Gulf, naming it "Thessaloniki" ("Thessalian victory") after his wife; he also rebuilt Thebes, which Alexander had leveled in 335 B.C.

Antigonus the One-Eyed meanwhile attempted to gain total control of the empire against the allied forces of Cassander, Ptolemy, and Lysimachus. Seleucus captured Babylon from Antigonus in 312 B.C., and the following year a temporary peace was agreed to among the successors.

In 310 B.C., Roxanne and Alexander IV were murdered by Cassander, Antigonus, and his son, Demetrius I *Poliorkitos* (the "Besieger"). These men subsequently declared themselves the royal successors to Alexander.

War broke out between Cassander and Demetrius for control of Greece in 307 B.C. Demetrius besieged and took Athens, but later failed to conquer Rhodes. Ptolemy and Seleucus declared themselves kings of their territories in 305 B.C. and established their respective dynasties. Thus came to an end all pretense of honoring Alexander's dream of a unified empire.

In 301 B.C., Antigonus was killed at the battle of Ipsus (Phrygia) by the forces of Lysimachus and the other successors. Cassander died of natural causes in 298 B.C., freeing Demetrius the Besieger to take the kingdom of Macedonia. The following year, Demetrius was attacked by Lysimachus and Pyrrhus of Epirus, and then by Seleucus. Finally captured by the latter in 285 B.C., Demetrius drank himself to death. Lysimachus turned on Pyrrhus and drove him out of the territory a year later. Lysimachus crowned himself king of Macedonia.

In Egypt, Ptolemy died and was succeeded by his son, Ptolemy II.

By 282 B.C., the spreading power of Rome had taken all of the Greek colonies in Italy except Tarentum, which appealed to the virtually homeless Pyrrhus of Epirus for help. He sailed for Italy in 280 B.C. with twenty-five thousand men and twenty elephants and victoriously engaged the Romans at the battle of Heracleia. But immense losses led to Pyrrhus' retreat from Italy and eventual defeat by the Romans in Epirus five years later. Hence, the term "Pyrrhic victory."

Meanwhile, Lysimachus had been killed in battle by the forces of Seleucus in 281 B.C. Seleucus, in turn, was assassinated while attempting to take Macedonia; he was succeeded by his son, Antiochus I.

Thus ended the Age of the Successors.

Alexander's empire was now divided between by the Ptolemaic and Seleucid dynasties to the south and east and, on the Greek mainland, by the Greeks themselves (particularly Sparta and the Achaean League). It would be fought over until Rome's mighty war machine was freed from its battles with Hannibal and Carthage in 202 B.C.

Arts and Sciences

Because the cultural and scientific-philosophical developments of the Classical Age were so monumental (in every sense of the word), the accomplishments of the Hellenistic Age remain largely unknown to the general public — lost on that hazy bridge of happenings between the death of Alexander and the love affair of Antony and Cleopatra.

Part of this is also due to a diaspora of thinkers and artists that preceded the decline of Athens in the fourth century B.C. and the subsequent warring among Alexander's successors. This latter event fragmented society and fostered a strong sense of individual survival, which was reflected in the very personalized portraiture and sculpture of the period, as well as in its Cynic, Stoic, and Epicurean philosophies.

Due to the cultural unity of an empire in which Greek was now the common tongue (*koine*) of learning, commerce and diplomacy nevertheless flourished. So did the arts and the sciences, which were greatly stimulated by renewed contact with Oriental influences. This influence was particularly dominant in Alexandria, which the Macedonian Ptolemy had made the capital of Egypt. With its massive *museum* ("Home of the Muses") and library, Alexandria was considered second only to Athens as a seat of learning and culture. At the same time, Alexandria was the predominant center of Hellenistic scientific activity.

Athens still possessed some of its old glory, however, and a number of personages in the arts and sciences decided to stay there in spite of its waning influence. Among these was the philosopher Diogenes (*c.* 412–323 B.C.). Considered the founder of the Cynic school of philosophy, he fostered a complete disregard for creature comforts. Thus, he ate plain food, slept outside, and stood bearded on street corners, sneering at the clean-shaven, wealth-oriented new class of Athenian citizen.

Legend has it that Diogenes also wandered through the city with a lantern, looking for an honest man. He once met Alexander while sunbathing in Corinth. "Can I do anything for you?" asked Alexander. "Yes," said Diogenes, "you can get out of my light." This response prompted Alexander to say to friends, "If I were not Alexander, I would like to be Diogenes." According to yet another tradition, Diogenes died on the same day as Alexander, in 323 B.C.

At about the same time, Zeno (*c.* 335-236 B.C.) of Citum arrived in Athens and founded a school of philosophy, which advocated Reason as the faculty by which man can place himself in harmony with a predetermined universe. Because Zeno lectured in a colonnade (*stóa*), the philosophy became known as "Stoicism."

In 306 B.C., Epicurus of Samos opened a school in Athens in a walled garden. He promulgated the doctrine (later known as "Epicureanism") that happiness is to be found in withdrawing from political life, and cultivating in your own "garden" a serenity of mind and body by striving for an absence of pain.

Menander (*c.* 342–291 B.C.), the greatest of the Athenian "New Comedy" (of manners) playwrights, flourished in the same period. A friend of Epicurus, he had a grace and style that was deepened by compassion. "He whom the gods love," he wrote, "dies young." Although he authored over one hundred plays, only fragmented versions of the originals have survived — most notably *Dyskolos* (*The Grouch*) and *The Curmudgeon*. The other works are known only through the adaptations of the Roman playwrights, Terrence and Plautus. Menander is believed to have drowned while swimming in Piraeus.

In the meantime, Ptolemy I attracted an impressive number of thinkers to Egypt. He established the great museum-library of Alexandria (eventually to hold over a half million papyrus scrolls) in 300 B.C. Its first librarian, Zenodatus of Ephesus, immediately began a compilation of authentic *Iliad* and *Odyssey* texts. Euclid was in Alexandria at the same time, hard at work on his textbook of geometry, *The Elements*. In its complete form, the book summarizes the work of Euclid's mathematical predecessors — Pythagoras, Hippocrates of Chios, Eudoxos, and later Athenian and Pythagorean geometers — and includes his own original work on higher mathematics. In the same year, the famous *Pharos* (lighthouse), one of the Seven Wonders of the World, was built in Alexandria.

In other parts of Alexander's former empire, the *Colossus of Rhodes* was being built to bestride the entrance of the island's harbor; and in the Seulucidian capital of Antioch, the sculptor Eutychides was creating his *Tyche*.

Hellenistic science and culture flourished in the stability that preceded the end of the Wars of the Successors and lasted until the Romans began their conquest of Greece.

In 280 B.C., the philosopher Strato succeeded Theophrastus as head of Aristotle's Lyceum and posited the doctrine that "nature abhors a vacuum." He would be the Lyceum's last head, as it would close upon his death in 269 B.C.

At about this time, Aristarchus of Samos theorized that the earth revolved around the sun; and Erasistratus of Ceos, an Alexandrian physiologist, explained the workings of the circulatory system and the motor and sensory nerves, and suggested preventive medicine through diet, hygiene, and exercise.

Also active during this period (260–212 B.C.) was Archimedes of Syracuse, a mathematician and inventor. His many accomplishments include determining the value of PI (p), discovering the law of floating bodies, and learning how to measure specific gravity. Archimedes was killed during the Roman siege of Syracuse by a soldier too impatient to wait for his conclusion of a mathematical problem etched in the sand.

Apollonius of Rhodes, successor to Zenodotus as the librarian at Alexandria, lost his job upon the succession of Ptolemy III to the throne in *c.* 250 B.C. The ex-librarian then retired to Rhodes, where he wrote the *Argonautica* about Jason's quest for the

Golden Fleece. In the same year, the *Laocoön* — a Trojan priest punished by the gods for trying to warn against gift-bearing Greeks — was sculpted in Rhodes by Agesander, Polydorus, and Athenodorus. In Athens, the Stoic philosopher Ariston of Chios was active.

In 246 B.C., Eratosthenes was appointed head of the Alexandria Library and also correctly calculated the circumference of the earth.

An earthquake toppled the *Colossus of Rhodes* in 239 B.C., while another quake devastated the island in 225 B.C.

The great library of Perganum was founded in 196 B.C. as the only serious rival to that of Alexandria; in the same year, the Rosetta Stone was carved, describing the coronation of Ptolemy V in hieroglyphics as well as Greek and demotic characters. Upon the latter's unearthing in 1799, it would provide the key for the decipherment of Egyptian hieroglyphics.

In 190 B.C., the *Farnese Bull* was sculpted at Caria. Other famous sculptures of the Hellenistic period include the *Dying Gaul* (now at Rome), the *Venus de Milo*, and the *Nike of Samothrace* (both in the Louvre in Paris) — all great works of art, but Baroque-like embellishments nevertheless on the great, pure directness that was the Renaissance of the Classical Period.

THE ROMAN DOMINATION

Rome's defeat of Hannibal and Carthage finally enabled it to turn its attention eastward, particularly towards Philip V of Macedonia, who had allied himself with Carthage, and whose armies were weakened by decades of internecine battles between the Successors and attacks by other Greek city-states.

In a series of three Macedonian Wars from 215–168 B.C., the Romans gradually gained control of Macedonia. The death knell of the beleaguered empire was the resounding defeat of Philip V's successor, Perseus, at the battle of Pydna in 168 B.C. Perseus fled to the famous sanctuary on the Thracian island of Samothrace, but was subsequently captured by the Romans. To weaken the defeated Macedonian empire, Rome divided it into four territories and then focused on the rest of Greece.

Having suppressed the Achean League, sacked Corinth, and quelled a Macedonian revolt, Rome made Greece a provincial territory by 146 B.C. With the Via Egnatia now constructed between Rome and the Macedonian capital of Thessaloniki, the province of Greece was administered in the latter city. Athens was accorded a special status under this administration.

A period of peace then followed.

In the meantime, the dynamism of Rome had started to attract artists and thinkers from all over Alexander's former empire. Carneades, head of Plato's academy, brought philosophy to the city in 155 B.C. Polybius, an Arcadian Greek, retired from the Roman government seven years later in order to write a history of Rome's rise to prominence from 221–146 B.C. The city's status as a cultural center was further accentuated in 145 B.C., when Ptolemy VIII ascended to the Egyptian throne and drove artists and scholars out of Alexandria.

The long-standing peace of the Grecian province was broken in 88 B.C. when Mithradites VI, King of Pontus (along the southern coast in the Black Sea), attacked Roman territories in the east with Athenian support. Two years later, Roman troops under Sulla sacked Athens, shipped most of its artwork back to Rome, and razed the Long Walls of Piraeus.

After a three-year siege, the Romans finally captured Crete in 67 B.C.; one year later, Pompey defeated Mithradites on the way to ending the Seleucid Dynasty in 64 B.C.

Cleopatra and the Last Stand of Alexander's Successors

While the affairs of Cleopatra, political and otherwise, appear to stand outside the province of Greek history, the fact that she was of Macedonian descent and that so many of her later decisive battles took place on Greek soil thoroughly justifies her inclusion. Hers is also, as always, a fascinating story.

Upon the death of her father, eighteen-year-old Cleopatra was made co-ruler of Egypt along with her twelve-year-old brother, Ptolemy XIII. Three years later, she was driven into exile by a faction associated with her brother. Appealing to Julius Caesar for support, she became his lover and was restored to the throne in 47 B.C. when he proclaimed her Queen of Egypt. Later that year, she gave birth to Caesarion, who is believed to have been Caesar's son.

Meanwhile, a civil war had been raging in the Roman Empire between Caesar and Pompey. During one battle in Alexandria, the Great Library was burnt down, resulting in the incomparable cultural loss of the sole copies of thousands of manuscripts, particularly those of Greece's Classical Age writers and thinkers.

At the same time, the territory of Hermaeus in northwest India had passed under the suzerainty of China. Thus ended the era of Greek kingship in the area.

In 44 B.C., Caesar was murdered and Brutus went into self-exile in Macedonia. Brutus and Cassius committed suicide two years later, after having been defeated by Antony in two battles at Philippi.

Antony summoned Cleopatra to Rome in 41 B.C. to demand her explanation as to why she had not allied herself with Caesar during the civil wars. In the process, Antony began to fall in love with her. They then returned together to Egypt. In 40 B.C., however, he was compelled by political exigency to go back to Rome and marry Octavia — the sister of Caesar's nominal successor, Octavian. The subsequent Pact of Brundesium granted Antony Rome's eastern provinces. During this period, Cleopatra gave birth to twins, presumably his children.

Antony and Cleopatra met again in 37 B.C. He "married" her a year later, giving her his Roman territories in the east. But in 32 B.C., the Roman senate declared war on Cleopatra, depriving Antony of all authority. He and Cleopatra were defeated by Octavian at the battle of Actium (near present-day Lefkadia), and returned to Egypt. As Octavian was about to invade Alexandria in 30 B.C., Antony killed himself upon receiving a false report that Cleopatra was dead. She in turn committed suicide, as

Cleopatra and her son, Caesarion, as Isis and Horus. On the outside wall of the temple of Hathor at Denderah.

Bust of Mark Antony.

legend would have it, from the bite of an asp. Octavian executed Caesarion, thereby ending the Ptolemy Dynasty and making Egypt a Roman province.

One year later, the Greek geographer Strabo toured Greece and noted the great devastation caused by the Roman civil wars. He then wrote an enormous history of the country that was intended to succeed Polybius' history. Unfortunately, only fragments of Strabo's forty-three volumes have survived. However, his *Geography* — seventeen volumes detailing the world as it was then known — has survived almost *in toto*.

Octavian, given the title "Augustus," became caesar of the new Imperial Roman Empire in 27 B.C., and immediately imposed the famous *Pax Romana*.

THE *PAX ROMANA* AND THE RISE OF CHRISTIANITY

This period saw Greek language and culture exercise a considerable influence on the Roman world, taking its territories much as Rome's armies had taken Greece — by storm. The Greek language was also, as a result of Alexander's conquests and the Hellenization of these territories by his successors, playing a vital role in the east-west dissemination of a new religion that would later seem to be to many Greeks a part of their native heritage: Christianity. One need only be apprised of the fact that Jesus' appellation, "messiah," is *christós* in Greek to understand how intimately Christianity and Greek culture have been intertwined.

In 49 B.C.E., the Apostle Paul arrived in Greece at Neapolis (present-day Kavala in Macedonia) to begin his first missionary journey through the country. The fluent Greek-speaker was accompanied by a "man from Macedonia," perhaps St. Luke the Physician. Paul traveled to Philippi (where an earthquake freed him from prison), Thessaloniki, Veria, and Athens, where he spoke before the Council of the Areopagus.

From 50–51 he was in Corinth, where he wrote the First Letter to the Thessalonians, the oldest document in the New Testament. Paul then returned to Antioch via Ephesus. In 57 58, he went back to Macedonia and Corinth before returning to the Middle East.

On the way to Rome by ship in 61, a storm forced Paul to land on the southern coast of Crete at Kaloi Limenes. He continued on to Rome sometime later, perhaps returning to Crete one final time (at Gortyna) before his martyrdom by decapitation on the road to Ostia outside of Rome.

The Four Gospels were written down in the popular Greek (*koine*) of Alexander's empire in the years 60–120. In *c.* 95, St. John was exiled to the Greek island of Patmos (near Ephesus), where he received and transcribed the Book of Revelations. Also during this period, the Apostle Peter and the Virgin Mary were shipwrecked on a peninsula of Chalkidiki, which the latter loved so much that she proclaimed it her personal garden. (As a result, no other females, not even hens, are allowed today in the monastic environs of Mt. Athos.) The Greek moralist Epictetus was also active at this time.

In the years 105–115, *Parallel Lives* was written and published by Plutarch (*c.* 46–120?), a Greek of ancient Theban ancestry. Plutarch's active contemporaries include the historian Appian and the satirist Lucian, both of whom wrote in Greek.

Also present in Rome was the Greek physician and philosopher Galen (*c.* 129–199), the single greatest figure in medicine after Hippocrates. Galen was the personal physician to Marcus Aurelius and the author of some four hundred works, many of which became the standard texts on anatomy and bodily functions for the following fourteen hundred years.

From 160 to 180, the Greek geographer and historian Pausanias traveled in central and southern Greece and wrote accounts of these journeys, which depict a country far better off than in Strabo's time but still poor and fallen. Pausanias' books remain invaluable guides to archaeologists in search of ancient sites.

The first incursions of new barbarian tribes from the north occurred in 175, when the Costoboci broke into central Greece and briefly ended the Roman peace. In 250, the Goths captured and sacked Athens before they were pushed back beyond the Danube. The Heruli invaded from the Black Sea area in 267 and burned both Ephesus and Athens.

At this time, the Roman philosopher Plotinus was writing the *Enneads* in Greek. Based on Plato's theory of Ideas, they espouse a mystical, Neoplatonist concept of a single Absolute Being — the One, from which everything else flows and with which, through thought and purification of the senses, it is possible to achieve an ecstatic union. Strains of this philosophy would later have an important influence on many areas of Christianity, particularly on the development of the Greek Orthodox Church.

ROME'S DECLINE AND FALL

Increasing pressure by barbarians on its border areas caused a shift of men, goods, money, and power to the peripheries of the Roman Empire — a situation that created excessive bureaucracy and rampant inflation and corruption. To combat these problems, the emperor Diocletian (284–305) re-instituted the divine power of his office, using it to overhaul and restructure the entire empire in order to bring control of its immense territory more firmly into the hands of its rulers. His principal innovation was to split the empire's administration into four regions in 293. In each region there were two *caesars* or *augusti*, with the four together known as the *Tetrarchy*; Diocletian, however, retained ultimate supremacy over these administrators. He then established his seat at Nicodemia, near the ancient town of Byzantium on the Bosphorus.

Diocletian retired in 305 and forced one of the other caesars, Maxentius, to do likewise, leaving power in the hands of the remaining two *caesars*: Galerius in the east, and Constantius in the west. This co-rulership did not prove amicable and, after their deaths, there were four contenders for power. Two of these were sons of men who had ruled in the *Tetrarchy*: Maxentius, son of Maximian, and Serbian-born Favius Valerius Constantinus (later revered as Constantine the Great), son of Constantius.

Constantine and Maxentius confronted each other across the Tiber in 312, on the eve of a decisive battle for the throne. At this moment, Constantine was said (by Eusebius, a contemporary and official historian of the Christian church) to have seen a cross manifest itself in the sky. It was accompanied by the exhortation, "In this sign, conquer." Constantine did just this the following day, becoming undisputed emperor in the west. While he was moved by this visitation to become a patron and protector to his Christian subjects, Constantine did not become a Christian until he was baptized on his deathbed in 337.

Constantine and a co-emperor, Licinius, issued the Edict of Milan, legitimizing Christianity within the empire in 313. Troubled by the fashionability of their religion, certain priests began to withdraw into remote places such as Cappadocia and the Egyptian desert as a reminder to themselves and society that God's kingdom was not of this world. These were the first Christian monks.

After vanquishing Licinius and the other co-emperor of the east, Constantine established himself as the sole ruler of the entire Roman Empire in 323. Immediately, he began searching for a new capital far away from the intrigues of Rome. After considering Jerusalem and Illium, he received another sign from God in 324 that prompted him to select the little town of Byzantium as the new capital.

Constantine summoned and presided over the Council of Nicea in 325, the first Ecumenical Council of the Christian Church. Its purpose was to establish a firm basis and agreed-upon content of Christianity within the empire. The council produced the Nicene Creed, which denies the Arian contention that Jesus was a created being less than God and states the belief that Jesus was "one in essence with the Father."

Constantine's mother, a former Christian servant girl afterwards celebrated as St. Helena, went on a pilgrimage to the Holy Land in 327, where she was believed to have unearthed the True Cross at Jerusalem.

In 330, Constantine inaugurated the city of New Rome, also known as in Greek Constantinople (the *pólis* of Constantine), and ushered in the 1122-year era of the Byzantine Empire.

BYZANTIUM

With Constantinople one of the two capitals of a still undivided empire and Christianity its official religion in all but name, the Byzantine Empire developed as a fusion of three cultural strains: in the realm of politics, law, and the military, the empire was Roman; in the realm of literature and language, it was Greek; and, due to Alexander's Hellenization of the East, the realm of religion and the language of the Gospels were also Greek.

With the continuing decline of Athens, the center of Greek civilization and, in effect, the geographical center of Greece, was thus shifted to Constantinople. Greeks even today call it *ee Pólis* ("the City" — i.e., the one and only city) or *Constantinópoli*, the Turkish appellation "Istanbul" having been derived from the local Greek words *stan pólin*, which mean "in (at, to) the city." In addition, many present-day Greeks also refer to themselves as *Romioi* (Romans), subjects of the Eastern Orthodox Roman Christian Empire, as opposed to the standard designation *Élleness* with its pagan origins and connotations.

Hence, to a Greek, any history of Greece that did not include the history of the Byzantine Empire would be, to say the least, blasphemously incomplete.

The Early Byzantine Age

Perhaps waiting until the last possible moment to receive what was then believed to be a one-time-only chance to be absolved of

106

sins, Constantine was baptized as a Christian on his deathbed in 337.

After a brief return to paganism from 360–363 under the emperorship of Julian the Apostate, Christianity was unofficially restored before the Byzantine emperor Theodosius proclaimed it the official state religion in 380. The following year, the Second Ecumenical Council developed the Nicene Creed and the concept of the Trinity, stressing the point that the Holy Spirit "proceeds from the Father" only — a distinction that would be the main theological cause of the schism between the Roman and Eastern churches in 1054.

Theodosius then issued proclamations in 392 that closed all heathen temples, including the Parthenon (subsequently dedicated to the Virgin Mary as the "place of the virgins"), Delphi, and Olympia. Afterwards, he forbade the Olympic games because of their nudity.

When Theodosius died in 395, his sons Honorius and Arcadius partitioned the empire into autonomous western and eastern halves, respectively, and ended Imperial Roman unity. In 476, after repeated sackings by northern invaders, Rome (and with it, the Western Empire) fell to the Visigoths.

From 527–565, the man who is thought of as the last of the great Roman emperors, Justinian I, ruled Byzantium along with his remarkable wife, the actress and courtesan Theodora. During this period, the Byzantine Empire assumed its distinctive eastern, as opposed to Roman, form. The fire-damaged Church of Hagia Sophia ("Holy Wisdom") was rebuilt in its symbolically opulent and magisterial final form, complete with the True Cross of Jesus, His swaddling clothes, and the table of the Last Supper — all of

107

The interior of St. Sophia. Mosaics of Emperor Justinian and Empress Theodora.

St. Sophia today with added Turkish minarets.

which were brought back from Jerusalem by the empress Helena. In 529, the closing of Plato's Academy signaled the complete shift of Greek culture and its heritage from Athens to Constantinople. Finally, during the reign of the emperor Heraclitus (610–641), Greek was declared the official language of the empire.

The Middle Byzantine Age

This age was characterized by two enormous dangers to the continuance of the empire: the sudden explosion of Islamic armies out of the Arabian peninsula, which threatened the very gates of Constantinople in 637 and reduced the Byzantine Empire to a predominately Greek core; and internal conflicts between the Iconoclasts ("icon smashers," which they often literally were) and Iconodules ("icon venerators"), which raged with great periodic violence for over 120 years (726–843) and threatened the doctrinal heart of the Orthodox Church.

The icon controversy hinged on two questions: whether or not icon veneration represented idolatry; and whether the Orthodox concept of the human aspect of divinity as embodied by Jesus did or did not give human beings the spiritual power to depict this divinity through their art and thus participate in the redemption of the world.

The icon venerators ultimately won, and their final victory in 843 is still celebrated as "Orthodox Sunday," on the first day of Lent.

Elsewhere during this period:

Charlemagne's coronation in 800 signaled the revival of Western religious and military power as manifested by the Holy

Roman Empire, as well as the deepening division between East and West.

In 860, two Orthodox monks from Thessaloniki who would later be canonized, the brothers Cyril and Methodius, devised the Cyrillic alphabet in order to translate the Bible into Slavonic for missionary journeys to convert pagans in the north. Ultimately, the number of converts gained in Russia was so great that the country became the bastion of Orthodoxy following the fall of Constantinople to the Ottomans in 1453.

In 867, the Byzantine emperor Basil I founded his great Macedonian dynasty, which established Byzantine hegemony over virtually all of the Balkan Peninsula. After destroying the Bulgarian army, Basil II made a significant, triumphal march through all of Greece in 1018 — a march that ended with a ceremony in the Parthenon's Church of the Virgin Mary celebrating Byzantine dominance. The dynasty ended with the death of Basil II in 1025.

In 1054, the Roman and Eastern Churches, gradually separated over the centuries by foreign armies and diverging languages, made their final break. Each excommunicated the other on the basis of two issues: Papal claims to absolute rather than relative authority; and the Roman Catholics' insertion of a clause in the Nicene Creed stating that the Holy Spirit proceeded not only from the Father but also from the Son. The latter was a delicate but important theological point which the Orthodox believed upset the human side of the balance in the Holy Trinity and, subsequently, the human workings of the Spirit in the world.

One year later, the Seljuk Turks took Jerusalem and Baghdad, the seat of the Arab caliphate, and began raiding other Byzantine territories. The Normans, meanwhile, encroached on Byzantine territory in Italy. In 1071, at the battles of Bari in Italy and Manzikert in Armenia, the Byzantines lost all of Italy to the Normans and almost all of Asia to the Seljuk Turks.

The Destruction of Byzantium

As the Normans invaded Greece in 1081, Alexius I Comnenus became the Byzantine emperor. He established the Comneni dynasty and began a vigorous defense of the empire.

In response to the Arab takeover of the Holy Land, the First Crusade headed eastward from Europe to retake Jerusalem — a goal it successfully accomplished in 1099. The Second Crusade was launched in 1147, but did not prove so single-minded. In passing, the Normans attacked and took Corfu, Corinth, and Thebes from the Byzantines. The Third Crusade was officially undertaken in response to the capture of Jerusalem by the Moslems under Saladin in 1187. During the expedition, however, the German king Barbarossa, in a revealing moment, threatened but did not attack Constantinople.

From 1201–1204, the combined armies of the Fourth Crusade looted, burned, and desecrated the city. The Venetian-led forces took with them, among innumerable priceless items, the famous lions and bronze horses later installed in the Piazza San Marco in Venice. Constantinople subsequently came under Latin, primarily Frankish, control, while members of the Byzantine court fled to create principalities at Epirus and Nicaea in western Anatolia, as well as throughout the Black Sea region. The

The Bronze Horses of St. Mark outside the basilica of St. Mark, Venice.

Venetians took Crete in 1210 and began a 465-year occupation of the island.

In 1261, the Nicean ruler, Michael VIII Paleologus, retook Constantinople from the Franks and established the last Byzantine dynasty: the Paleologi. These kings ruled over a severely weakened empire racked by civil wars, plague, poverty, and foreign invasions; yet, it was radiant with a last flush of feverish artistic brilliance that was fueled, as the mind of the dying often is, by memories of its own past — in this case, the richness and humanism of its Classical Greek heritage.

Thus, while the empire was slowly expiring, artworks of the highest order were being created by many anonymous craftsmen, as well as by some whose names have since become celebrated. Among the latter group are the brilliant Russian icon painter, Reublev, and the great Cretan painter of frescoes, Theophanes the Greek.

In 1301, the Seljuk Empire collapsed under the pressure of Mongol invasions led by Genghis Khan. A small Turkish emirate in northwestern Anatolia then began its rise to dominance under Osman, founder of the Ottoman dynasty, with the defeat of a Byzantine force outside Nicomedia, across the Sea of Marmara from Constantinople.

From 1326–1397, beginning with the cities of Asia Minor, the Ottoman Turks gradually took all of the Byzantine Empire (and the Serbian empire as well) except for the Morea in the Peloponnese, some small territory northwest of Constantinople, and the city itself. Before the Turks could attack the Byzantine capital, they were attacked in the east by Mongols under Tamberlane. The Turks returned to besiege Constantinople in 1422, but were again turned back by outside forces — this time, a revolt in Ankara.

From 1444–1448, two final Crusades were instigated by the Roman Pope in order to save Byzantium from the "barbarians." Both armies, however, were crushed by the Turks.

In 1453, from April 6 to May 29, the Turks besieged and took Constantinople. Constantine XI Paleologus, the last of the Byzantine emperors, leapt into the battle and was never seen again. In the church of Hagia Sophia, the priests were murdered at the altar as they celebrated matins. It is said that one or two escaped into the walls of the church with the Eucharist plates and chalices, vowing to remain there until Constantinople was restored to the Christians – i.e., the Greeks. The service would then resume where it had been interrupted.

THE OTTOMAN OCCUPATION

This 400-year period saw the see of the Greek Orthodox Church become the principal repository and keeper of the identity of the Greeks as a people and as a nation, despite the Turkish occupation of its Holy City. This fact was in no small part due to the tenets of Islam, which looked upon Jesus as a prophet and upon the Bible as a holy book. The Turks therefore considered the Christians to be "People of the Book," who should be allowed freedom of worship, so long as they did not try to overthrow or desecrate Islam and its power.

On the other hand, the secular officials of Islam made certain that the Christians would never for a moment forget their second-class status. Accordingly, the government kept the Christian Church and its adherents heavily shackled with taxes and various rules and regulations.

One of these rules, however, was that the Orthodox Church should also be an administrative body seeing to the secular affairs of its flock, effectively making the Patriarch the political head of the Greek nation.

In addition, the Ottomans handed much of the local administration in Greece proper over to the leading Greek citizens (*árhondes*) of the towns and villages — an arrangement that further helped in the preservation of a Greek national identity.

Thus, while the Greeks and their lands became subject to the Ottoman Empire, their hearts, minds, and souls remained relatively free — albeit in a kind of purgatory — and managed to survive the occupation with their essential Greekness unaltered.

In 1648, the Turks began a siege to take Iraklion (Candia), the capital of Crete, from the Venetians. Iraklion fell in 1669, and the Turks occupied the entire island.

In 1683, however, the Turks failed in their second attempt to take Venice — an occasion celebrated with the invention of the croissant in the shape of the Turkish crescent by a Viennese baker. This failure effectively ended any further attempts on the part of the Ottoman Empire to expand their territory.

The following year, war broke out between Venice and the Ottoman Empire. From 1686–1715, the Venetian admiral Francesco Morosini conducted his Odyssean expedition throughout Ottoman-occupied Greece. During one of these journeys, he besieged Athens (1687) and led the troops who fired upon the Parthenon, which had been converted to a Moslem mosque. The landing shells touched off explosives stored inside the Parthenon and blew out its roof and interior walls, leaving it in the approximate condition it is today.

The Rise of Greek Nationalism

The last half of the eighteenth century saw the Ottoman Empire's decline, which resulted from the following: military, political, and espionage pressure from Russia; wide-ranging rampages by Albanian warlords on the Greek mainland; and an internal lack of will, as the increasingly decadent sultanate handed more and more of their administrative affairs over to educated Greeks from the Phanar area of Constantinople, who then received the appellation "Phanariotes."

117

Morosini's shelling of the Acropolis with Turkish ammunition stored inside (1687).

In the meantime, active resistance by Greeks within the empire was encouraged and financed by expatriate Greeks in Russia and the West, as well as by non-Greek sympathizers, generally called "Philellenes" or "Friends of Greece." One of the results was the organization of a secret society, the *Filikí Etería* ("Society of Friends") in Odessa in 1814. Operated by agents inside and outside the country, its purpose was to organize resistance against the Turks and prepare for the long-anticipated uprising against them.

A romantic and intellectual grass-roots movement to free the Greeks was gaining ground among the educated in Europe. Its adherents believed that the glory of Greece still resided in its modern descendants and that to liberate the cradle of democracy from the Turkish yolk was an almost sacred duty. The movement became a crusade approached with all the fervor (and, on a political level, the opportunism) of the earlier ones to Jerusalem. Of course, it had little to do with the idea of their identity held by the modern Greeks, who thought — and still think — of themselves more as children of Byzantium and the Orthodox Church than of Classical Greece.

As the nineteenth century began, there was a parallel effort undertaken by other "Friends of Greece" to locate and "liberate" ancient Greek art treasures from Ottoman hands — sometimes to truly save them, as was apparently the case with the Elgin Marbles, and sometimes simply to acquire them. Needless to say, these activities were executed with the eager cooperation of Turkish officials, who were given much-needed foreign currency in exchange for allowing the pillage.

In 1800, Lord Elgin of Great Britain purchased sculpted marble sections from the frieze and tympani of the Parthenon, which had been damaged by the Morosini explosion. It is said that he acquired these pieces, most of which were sculpted by the Greek master Phideas, in order to save them from being pulverized into marble by the Turks. They were subsequently purchased by the British government in 1816 and installed in the British Museum.

The British poet Lord Byron made his first visit to Greece in 1809–1811, where he called on the Ottoman-allied Albanian warlord, Ali Pasha, in Epirus. Lord Byron journeyed to Athens

Lord Byron arriving in Mesolongi on January 4, 1824.

and Constantinople, swam the Hellespont, toured the Peloponnese, and finally returned to Athens to work on his first major poetic success, *Childe Harold's Pilgrimage*, which is partly an account of these voyages. He also composed a poem, "The Curse of Minerva," that condemns the "pilfered prey" of Greek antiquities by Lord Elgin and others.

In 1814, the secret revolutionary society, the *Filikí Etería*, was founded in Odessa — a city first settled by the ancient Greeks in 630 B.C. and annexed by Russia in 1792. The Society moved its headquarters in 1818 to the very heart of the enemy but the very soul of modern Greece: Constantinople. There, it recruited various Greek notables, the most important of whom were the *bey* ("provincial governor") of the Mani area of the Peloponnese, Mavromichalis; the *klephtic* ("bandit") leader, Kolokotronis; and the Bishop of Patras, Germanos. The leadership of the society, after having been declined by John Capodistrias, was accepted by Alexander Ypsilantis, a Phanariot Greek officer in the Russian army.

As plans for a coordinated uprising continued, so too did the archaeological plundering. In 1820, on the island of Milos, a Hellenic statue of Aphrodite was uncovered by a farmer and quickly purchased by a French naval officer. The latter then took the statue to his homeland, where it was eventually housed in the Louvre as the "Venus de Milo."

The French, however, also had their hands in other matters. In the same year, with French backing, the Albanian warlord Ali Pasha, a perpetual loose cannon on the Ottoman ship of state, refused to accept the sultan's decree deposing him. As a result, the Ottomans sent a force of fifty thousand soldiers to his castle at Yanina in Epirus to subdue him.

While these two forces were preoccupied with one another, Ypsilantis made an ill-advised decision to raise the flag of revolution by leading a small army, including eight hundred students, from Russian into Ottoman territory. He naïvely hoped for spontaneous support from the Bulgarians, Romanians, and Serbs, not to mention Russia. But he received nothing, and the Turkish Jannisaries, allowed by the Russians to enter their territory, decimated the inexperienced Greek force on February 25, 1821.

A Greek sea captain (c. 1820).

The "Venus de Milo."

Nevertheless, news of Ypsilantes' rash but courageous attempt spread throughout Greece and ignited the flames of revolution in a way he had not even imagined — not from outside of Greece, but from within. A month after the defeat of the army, Bishop Germanos literally raised the flag of revolt against the Turks at the Monastery of Ayia Lavra in the northern Peloponnese. The date of March 25 is now celebrated as Greek Independence Day.

THE GREEK REVOLUTION

In 1821–1822, with the Turks occupied by the rebellion of Ali
Pasha, other internal strife, and threats from Russia and Persia,
the Greek rebels established footholds in the Peloponnese and
some Aegean islands. The Ottomans, in reprisal for the slaughter
of Turkish civilians in the Peloponnese, executed the Greek
Patriarch in Constantinople. Meanwhile, a provisional Greek
government under Alexandros Mavrokordatos was organized in
Epidauros; and, as European newspapers reported the uprisings,
many Europeans rushed to join the Greek cause.

But the momentum of the Greek rebellion was quickly
quashed by a savage Ottoman response. Beginning with the
hanging of the Patriarch on Easter Sunday of 1821, Ottoman
forces set out to crush and pre-empt the rebellion both outside
and inside Greece proper. They accordingly instituted a campaign of terror that resulted in a wholesale slaughter of Greek
civilians throughout the empire.

After finally defeating Ali Pasha through assassination
(sending his head to be displayed on a pole in the Seraglio), they
set about repressing the rebellion from the north of Greece south-
wards. At the battle for Nauplion in 1822, Ottoman forces became
overextended and, on their way back to Istanbul, were badly
mauled in an ambush set by Kolokotronis and his guerrillas. A
standoff ensued. The Turks pondered the problems of sending an
army to fight an essentially guerrilla war on the Greek mainland,
while the Greeks, as had been their history since arriving in the
area, fought among themselves. In their attempts to ensure an

The Greek Patriarch, Grigorios V, being hanged by the Turks in Constantinople three weeks after the revolution began in Greece.

advantage for their particular interest groups, families, and friends, they ended up fighting a virtual civil war within Greek-controlled areas — even as they continued to confront the Turks.

The Sultan called upon the Ottoman Pasha of Egypt for aid in 1823, offering the Greek-born Mehmet Ali the island of Crete (and his son, Ibrahim, the Peloponnese) in return for his help. The following year, Mehmet Ali's forces landed on Crete, and the Turks entered the Peloponnese from the north. However, they were subsequently pushed back to the other side of Corinthian Isthmus, where they then besieged Missolonghi. Lord Byron, who had arrived there the previous July with money and a regiment to help the Greeks, was made commander in chief of the Greek forces; but three months later, on April 19, 1824, he caught a fever and died. Meanwhile, a real civil war broke out between the Greek provisional government and the rebel leader Kolokotronis, who was ultimately defeated and imprisoned at Nauplion.

In January 1825, Ibrahim's forces, using Crete as a base, landed in the south of Peloponnese and moved northwards, crushing the rebellion everywhere except Nauplion. They joined the Turkish forces to successfully end the siege of Missolonghi.

The Greeks, desperate for help, released Kolokotronis from prison and reinstated him; but it seemed inevitable that without outside aid, the Greek revolution would be crushed by the combined forces of the Ottomans and Egyptians.

In July of 1827, Britain, Russia, and France, alarmed at the coalition of Egyptians and Turks that might leave most of Greece under Mehmet Ali's control, signed the tripartite Treaty of London. This pact threatened armed intervention if an armistice between the Greeks and the Turks was not signed. Though all sides ultimately agreed to an armistice, the hostilities did not cease. As a result, a tripartite navy of the Great Powers engaged and destroyed the Turkish-Egyptian fleet at the battle of Navarino on October 20, 1827.

Shortly thereafter, Mehmet Ali withdrew his forces, leaving the Peloponnese to the French. Russia then declared war on Turkey and, in the Russo-Turkish War of 1828–1829, took the Black Sea port of Varna. The Sultan signed a peace treaty at Adrianople on September 14, 1829, under the watchful eye of the Russian army, which also hoped to gain control of the Black Sea area and the entrance to the Mediterranean. In the meantime, the Greek Orthodox Church officially separated itself from the Patriarchy of Constantinople; rival national assemblies in free Greece agreed to the presidency of John Capodistrias, the Russian foreign minister who had previously turned down the leadership of the *Filikí Etería*.

From 1829–1832, to forestall each other's attempts to gain control of the region, the tripartite coalition engaged in negotiations to create a Kingdom of Greece. This task was made even more urgent after the authoritarian Capodistrias was assassinated by the *klephtic* chieftains of the Mani in the Peloponnese, Constantine and George Mavromichalis.

In May of 1832, King Ludwig I of Bavaria accepted the throne of the new Kingdom of Greece, a protectorate of the Great Powers, on behalf of his seventeen-year-old son, Otho. The Protocol of London thus declared independence for a country that did not yet include Crete, Thessaly, Macedonia, Thrace, Corfu, or the Ionian or Dodecanese islands.

MODERN GREECE: THE STRUGGLE FOR IDENTITY

Greece's struggle to forge its own identity in the modern world is a process that has yet to be completed, even though almost two hundred years have passed since its flag of revolution was first raised. This time has been marked by the continuing efforts of various political forces — both inside the country and out — to impose their respective visions of a "modern" Greece upon a people who have yet to completely break free from the mindset of four hundred years of Ottoman occupation. Coupled with this — in fact, inseparable from it — has been a vision and pursuit of a geographical identity, real and imagined, that would finally and ideally unite the two polar hearts of the Greek world and spirit: Athens and Constantinople.

Pursuing the "Great Idea": 1833–1912

In February of 1833, the Catholic King Otho I arrived in Nauplion to assume the throne of the new Kingdom of Greece. The Turks evacuated their garrison on the Acropolis one month later, thereby expediting the adoption of the dusty little (and entirely unsuited) village of Athens as the new Greek capital in 1834.

Archaeological expeditions continued in Ottoman-occupied territory. In 1839, French archaeologists in Thrace freed the "Winged Victory" of Samothrace from Turkish hands in order to permanently install it in the Louvre.

The Nike (Victory) of Samothrace at the Louvre.

With John Kolettis, Ali Pasha's ex-physician and the man who had imprisoned Kolokotronis, as prime minister and an autocratic Bavarian clique behind the throne, the government could not have been more unpopular with the Greek leaders of the revolution, and with the collection of rugged individualists that made up the populace. As a result, popular demonstrations backed by the army forced the king to grant a new constitution and elections in 1843. When the latter event was subverted by bribery and intimidation, and the appalling destitution among the people was left essentially unalleviated, pressures to topple Otho increased.

In the meantime, however, Kolettis proposed the "Great Idea": a greater Greece encompassing Constantinople and all the territories not yet acquired from the Ottomans. While it was a noble aspiration enthusiastically embraced by virtually all Greeks, as well as a politically astute diversion, it was entirely impractical in such a poverty-stricken country. As evidenced by the pressure it placed on leaders to take ill-advised military actions, and by the doomed uprisings it encouraged in occupied territories such as Crete, the "Great Idea" caused considerably more harm than good.

Otho himself attempted a disastrous invasion of Turkish territory in 1854, while the British, French, and other allies were helping the Turks fend off Russian acquisitiveness during the Crimean War. This affront to their ally, Turkey, so angered the British and French that they took control of the Greek government. Finally, following nationwide rebellions in 1862–1863, Otho I was taken out of the country by British warships.

The British then proposed the seventeen-year-old son of the King of Denmark as the new monarch and ceded the Ionian Islands to Greece as an incentive. In 1863, Prince William of Holstein-Sonderburg-Glucksburg was crowned as King George I. Another new constitution was adopted the following year, although little else initially changed.

In 1866, a group of rebelling Cretans, including women and children, blew themselves up inside the monastery at Arkadi rather than surrender to Ottoman soldiers. The new king of Greece and his government were moved to intervene, but were forcefully reminded by the Great Powers that they were beholden to them, not to the people of Greece. Threatened with severe reprisals if it attempted to help the Cretans and upset the existing balance of power, the government remained impassive.

Meanwhile, the great age of archaeological discoveries was gathering speed. In 1873, the German archaeologist Heinrich Schliemann realized his lifelong dream of unearthing Troy at His-arlik on the Turkish coast, mistakenly digging through the Troy of Homer's sage and labeling the gold he found the "Treasury of Priam." In 1876, he uncovered what he thought, again mistak-enly, were the tombs of "Agamemnon" and "Atreus" at Mycenae.

In 1875–1881, another team of German archaeologists exca-vated Olympia. Two years after this site's completion, a Cretan merchant found antiquities outside of Iraklion — a discovery that would lead to the discovery of the palace of Knossos in 1900. The merchant's first name, fittingly, was Minos.

At the same time, other interests started a feeding frenzy on the borders of the weakened Ottoman Empire. In 1875, the Serbs and Montenegrins attacked the Turks and were soon joined by the Russians. Greeks in Ottoman–occupied Epirus rebelled, and

Mycenaean gold death-mask mistakenly believed by Schliemann to be that of Agamemnon.

Crete once again joined them. But another quick settlement by the Great Powers continued to shore up the empire, and the Greeks gained nothing.

However, a convention of the Great Powers in 1881 granted most of Thessaly to Greece and, in doing so, restored the entire Greek mainland minus Epirus, Macedonia, and Thrace to the country.

Schliemann unearthed the palace and Cyclopean walls of Tiryns near Mycenae in 1884. Two years later, he visited Crete and tried to buy the land near Iraklion where the antiquities had been discovered. He failed and left the island in anger.

French archaeologists excavated Delphi in 1892–1903. On Crete, Sir Arthur Evans was working the land that Schliemann had been unable to buy; and, in 1900, he uncovered the great Minoan palace of Knossos.

On the modern political front, however, there were continuing frustrations over the pursuit of the "Great Idea," as Britain and France persisted in propping up the Ottoman Empire. At the same time, the disastrous financial situation within Greece was compelling many Greeks to emigrate overseas. The Greek Prime Minister Trikoupis declared Greece bankrupt in 1893.

In 1897, as the Cretans rose up and declared a provisional government at one end of the island, the Greek government could no longer restrain itself. It sent a fleet to Crete, while simultaneously invading Macedonia and Epirus to the north. The Ottomans came perilously close to taking Athens in a counterattack, but the Great Powers intervened and imposed a settlement. As had been the case with its predecessors, this pact re-instituted the status quo on both the mainland and Crete, although Crete was now declared to be under the care of an international protectorate.

In 1908, in Thessaloniki, a group of Turkish army officers known as the "Young Turks" rose up in insurrection against the Sultanate, with the intention of sweeping away the crumbling vestiges of the old regime and creating a modern Turkey. Although their revolution was quelled less than one year later, it nonetheless fueled the hopes of Greek nationalists who believed that, with dissension growing inside the Ottoman Empire, the realization of the "Great Idea" was indeed imminent.

With another frustrated uprising in Crete having again raised the stakes, and Ottoman Macedonia in danger of being subsumed by the Bulgarians, the Greek army staged a military coup in 1909. As a result, King George I was forced to depose his premier, Mavromichalis, in favor of Eleutherios Venizelos, the hero of the Cretan struggle for independence and one of the great statesmen of the twentieth century.

The following year, with his party having gained eighty percent of the seats in parliament — a consensus unmatched in Greek history, modern or ancient — Venizelos was able to push through many necessary tax, education, and property reforms. Armed with credentials as a bona fide leader of the Cretan uprisings, he could furthermore pursue the "Great Idea" with authority. He did just that during the Balkan Wars.

Eleutherios Venizelos compared with reverence to Christ.

The Balkan Wars: 1912–1913

The Italians, at war with Turkey over Tripoli and the possible occupation of Thessaloniki, were granted "temporary" occupancy of the Dodecanese Islands in 1911, including its southernmost capital of Rhodes. Meanwhile, once more emboldened to take part in the dismemberment of the empire, Serbia and Bulgaria signed a mutual defense pact recognizing each other's rights, but not the Greeks', in a division of Macedonia.

Venizelos had already begun to augment the Greek armed forces, however, and in a visit to London in 1912, forged a relationship with Lloyd George — a bond that would result in Greece being included, along with the Bulgarians, Serbs, and Montenegrins, in a Balkan League that would subsequently go to war against Turkey.

On October 12 of the same year, the First Balkan War began as the Montenegrins attacked Ottoman forces in Albania. One month later, the Greek army was in Thessaloniki; by the time the Treaty of London was signed ending the war in May of 1913, the Greeks had taken most of Macedonia and Epirus and declared Crete a part of the country. Venizelos forged a pact with the Serbs one month later that allied them against the Bulgarians, who had occupied Thrace.

When the Bulgarians attempted a pre-emptive strike against Serbia on June 30, the Second Balkan war erupted. By the time the war ended six weeks later, the Greeks had taken all of western Thrace up to Adrianopolis, where they had encountered an Ottoman army. Greece thus gained virtually all of its present-day territory, lacking only Mytilene and Chios. These territories would be annexed one year later, while the Dodecanese would continue to be occupied by the Italians until 1949.

Meanwhile, King George I had been assassinated in 1913 in Thessaloniki by a crazed loner. Constantine I, George's son, ascended to the throne, along with his pro-German sympathies. Therefore, while Britain, France, and Russia declared war on German-allied Turkey in the early days of the Great War, Greece initially remained neutral.

The First World War and Its Aftermath

In 1915, as Venizelos negotiated with the British to bring Greece into the war on the Allies' side, he was forced out of office by King Constantine, subsequently re-elected, and forced out again. While Venizelos formed a provisional second government in Thessaloniki in 1916–1917, the Allies imposed their will on Constantine by occupying northern Greece. Eventually, Constantine was pressured to abdicate in favor of his neutral younger son, Alexander. On June 27, 1917, Venizelos returned to Athens and severed diplomatic relationships with the Central Powers — the alliance of the German and Austro-Hungarian empires with Bulgaria and Turkey. Two days later, the Central Powers declared war on Greece.

By October, the Greek army was advancing towards Constantinople with British troops, relishing the possibility of being the first Greek soldiers to enter the city since its fall to the Ottomans in 1453. They never succeeded in reaching their destination, however, as Britain and Turkey abruptly signed an armistice.

The Versailles Peace Conference began in February of 1919. Venizelos pressured the Allies to grant the "concessions" in Asia Minor that Greece had been promised upon its entry into the war. Italy wanted similar promises fulfilled as well, and had sent warships to Smyrna (present-day Izmir) in anticipation of an occupation of the city. Venizelos persuaded the Allies to let him land troops there first, however, in order to protect the large Greek population in the city.

In November of the same year, the Peace Treaty of Neuilly between the Allies and Bulgaria granted western Thrace to Greece and allowed Bulgaria use of the Thracian port of Dedeagach, renamed Alexandroupouli.

In August 1920, the Peace Treaty of Sèvres between the Allies and Turkey (never ratified by the Turkish Assembly) granted Greece eastern Thrace (to within twenty miles of Constantinople), Smyrna, and the rest of the Aegean Islands except the Italian Dodecanese. These terms prompted the Thessaloniki-born Turkish general Mustafa Kemal Pasha, later known as Ataturk, to incite a revolution. He rallied enough opposition against the government to overthrow it and establish the modern Republic of Turkey, with its capital at Angora (now Ankara).

Heady with the opportunity to realize the "Great Idea" beyond even the most extravagant dreams of the Greeks, and campaigning for re-election on a platform of continued hostilities with Turkey, Venizelos ordered the Greek army to advance. He was voted out of office shortly afterwards, however, his fate having been sealed by two crucial factors: the intervening and accidental (some say) death of Alexander I due to a monkey bite; and the weariness of a public caught in what seemed to be an endless series of wars. Pacifist Royalist candidates thus came into power.

The Royalists immediately began a pattern of political revenge that has persisted in every change of government since. They purged the government, civil service, judiciary, and local governments of all Venizelist loyalists. With Venizelos in exile in France, the Royalists organized a plebiscite that returned Constantine I to power. They then resumed the war they promised not to enter into, but this time without the tacit support of either the French or British — neither of whom trusted Constantine. After warning the Greeks not to enter Constantinople, the Allies declared themselves neutral.

The Greco-Turkish War: 1921–1923

Initially, Greek troops advanced quickly across Asia Minor and Anatolia, coming to within twenty miles of the new capital of Ankara. But they had overextended themselves and, after suffering heavy losses in an attempt to break through the city's defenses, found themselves against the Aegean while neutral Allied warships stood offshore. There, the Greek army and hundreds of civilians were massacred on the quai at Smyrna by Turkish troops under the command of their new leader, Ataturk.

On September 8, 1922, an army coup d'etat forced Constantine I to abdicate. His eldest son ascended to the throne with the moniker of George II. This was approximately the same time as the formation of Greece's first Communist party, the pro-Moscow KKE.

In October, an armistice was agreed upon between Greece and Turkey, and the Greeks began to evacuate eastern Thrace. With the "Great Idea" in tatters and the consent of George II, the army in Athens court-martialed Prime Minister Gounaris and seven others for having lost the war. In a move sadly reminiscent of the Athenians' execution of their generals following the battle of Arginusae in 406 B.C., six Greek politicians and officers were shot by a firing squad.

In 1923, the Peace of Lausanne was signed, and eastern Thrace, Smyrna, and the islands of Imbros and Tenedos were returned to Turkey. The Italians kept the Dodecanese and, taking advantage of the turbulent times, seized Corfu. The British kept Cyprus.

Meanwhile, an immense exchange of populations had been agreed upon. Some 1.35 million Greeks and 430,000 Turks were subsequently resettled on the basis of their religion — adopted or not — after four hundred years of having been intermingled on two continents. The Patriarch of Constantinople and the 100,000 Greeks living in the city were allowed to remain, however, as were some Turks in western Thrace. The latter community would eventually be approved for citizenship, and still resides there today.

In that same year, Ataturk became the president of a deliberately secular (non-Islamic) Turkish republic.

Between the Wars

The years 1924–1935 were marked by a series of parliamentary struggles and military coup d'etats, in the midst of which the parliament named Greece a republic in 1924. Venizelos, in and out of office and the object of an assassination attempt in 1933, tried a coup d'etat himself in 1935. When it failed, he fled into exile in France via Italian-occupied Rhodes. George II, recalled by a rigged plebiscite, returned to Greece as monarch.

In 1936, Venizelos died in exile. At the same time, the Communists won fifteen seats in an inconclusive parliamentary election and thus held the balance of power between the Monarchists and Republicans. With the army manipulating events, George II named General Metaxas premier. He immediately abolished the constitution and, with the full accord of the king, became dictator of Greece. All political opposition was suppressed, as was anything tainted by democratic ideas, such as Sophocles' *Antigone* and Pericles' *Funeral Oration*.

General Metaxas, dictator of Greece (1936–1941).

World War II

In 1939, when war broke out in Europe, Metaxas proclaimed Greek neutrality in the hopes of remaining uninvolved. But Mussolini needed a whipping horse and concluded that he could get an easy victory in Greece. First, he invaded Albania. The following year, on August 15, 1940, Mussolini ordered a submarine to attack and sink the Greek cruiser *Elli* off the island of Tinos — an extreme act of provocation, particularly on a national holiday for the Assumption of the Virgin Mary whose focal point was the great cathedral there. Metaxas, however, restrained himself.

On October 28 of the same year, Metaxas was pushed to the breaking point. Following an Italian demand that he allow Mussolini's troops "right of passage" through Greece from Albania, Metaxas delivered his famous reply: *Ókhi!* ("No!") This date is now celebrated as a national holiday.

The Italians subsequently attacked, but the Greeks put up a fierce resistance. They were pushing the Italians back into Albania in 1941, when Metaxas suddenly died. His successor, General Papagos, allowed a British expeditionary force to land in Greece. The country thus became, in essence, Britain's only ally against the Nazis in Europe. Hitler immediately responded with bombardments and a full-scale invasion. Within a month, the Nazis had taken mainland Greece and signed an armistice with a puppet prime minister. Two weeks later, they conquered Crete, pushed the British out of the country, and forced King George and what was left of his government into exile in Cairo.

Various resistance groups continued to battle the Nazi occupation, however. Communists led the two largest and most popular of these groups: the National Popular Liberation Army (ELAS), which had been created simply to fight a people's war against the Nazis; and EAM, which was focused on both resisting the Nazis and, after the war was over, creating radical changes in the country's disastrous political structure. Neither party was initially allied with the Greek Community Party of the Exterior (i.e. allied to Moscow), the KKE. In fact, the latter viewed them both with some suspicion, particularly ELAS, which had potently arisen almost out of nowhere uncontrolled by any political party.

There were also a number of right wing groups, all of which were allied to former dictatorships and military factions. The most prominent of these was EDES, the National Republic Greek Army. It was this party that Churchill, greatly distrustful of any brand of communism, decided to support, along with the exiled Monarchist government. As a result, the British found themselves allied with groups that had virtually no support among the Greek people; and they had no share in a country that was, by 1944, under the divided control of ELAS and EAM, who were now fighting each other as much as the Nazis.

A British-backed "Government of National Unity" was nevertheless founded in Cairo, with an accomplished politician named George Papandreou at its head. A conference was held in Lebanon, from which ELAS abstained. There, Papandreou forged an agreement with the KKE and EAM to create a postwar government with several minor portfolios being given to the Communists. Although the EAM leaders in Greece, whose constituency was largely non-Communist, initially turned the offer down, Stalin ordered them to cooperate and wait for a more propitious moment to take over the country.

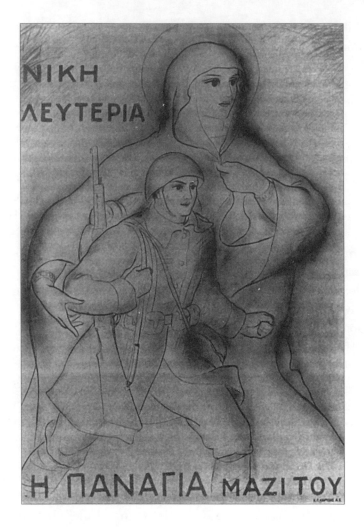

Propaganda poster from the Greek-Italian War of 1940–1941. The captions read: "Victory. Freedom. The Virgin Mary [is] with him."

Churchill with Athens Archbishop Damaskinos during the fighting between British troops and Communist resistance fighters of ELAS.

The British army landed in Patras and entered Athens in 1944. With ELAS refusing to turn in its arms, however, bitter fighting quickly broke out on the city's streets. One month later, a truce was negotiated; and in February 1945, under a promise of amnesty, the fighters of both EAM and ELAS turned in their arms. Shortly thereafter, the army, police, and right wing groups instituted a nationwide reign of terror against anyone connected with the Left. Thousands of people were arrested, hundreds were condemned to death, and countless others disappeared or were murdered. At the same time, some eighty thousand Greeks fled for their lives to the north where they took a stand with their backs to the borders of Communist Yugoslavia and Bulgaria.

Women resistance fighters, 1944.

The Greek Civil War: 1946–1949

By September 1946, when a plebiscite returned King George II to Greece, a terrible civil war between Communist and anti-Communist forces had erupted. The Truman Doctrine was proclaimed in March 1947 in order to buttress the Monarchist government against what seemed to be the danger of a Communist takeover. The United States provided $300 million in aid, as well as military advisors to assist the government-backed forces.

George II died this same year, and was succeeded by his brother, King Paul I.

In June and July of 1948, a major confrontation took place between government forces and the Communists on the slopes of Mt. Grammos between the borders of Greece and Albania. During the savage fighting, some twelve thousand partisan soldiers, believing that help would soon come from Yugoslavia, Bulgaria, and Russia, held off seventy thousand government soldiers equipped with tanks and airplanes for eight weeks.

Meanwhile, Tito and Stalin had reached an impasse. Stalin stuck to an agreement he had made with Churchill not to interfere in Greece, while Tito was unable to aid the partisans without Russian arms. Therefore, the partisans and their families were eventually forced to flee across the border. Simultaneously, thousands of children were rounded up, many of them forcibly taken from non-Communist families, and herded across the border to be trained as future fighters for the Communist cause.

Having definitively split with Moscow, Tito closed his border to the Greek Communists on July 10, 1949. With this act, the civil war came to an end. Many of the remaining partisans fled to

Albania and points north, while others hid in the mountains and remoter regions of Greece. The Communist Party was then outlawed and, with the Truman Doctrine triumphant, the United States replaced Britain as the principal foreign influence in Greece.

The Rule of the Right: 1950–1967

In 1952, after three years of chaos under a political system that, at one point, allowed as many as fifty-four parties to contend a general election, a new electoral system was devised with the aid of an American ambassador. With this system in place, the rightist Greek Rally Party so decisively won the next election that the Center and Left were momentarily rendered powerless and all but disenfranchised. This victory would lead to an uninterrupted but increasingly rocky fourteen years in power for the Right and its close Royalist allies. During this period, Greece and Turkey joined NATO in the widespread hope that their mutual membership in this defensive organization would keep them safe from communism, as well as from each other.

The Cyprus Question

But the Cyprus question emerged as a dangerous flashpoint between the two countries and within their internal politics. While Cyprus had never been a Greek possession, it had been home to a predominantly Greek-speaking population for centuries; in fact, the Greeks had colonized the island by *c.* 1400 B.C., and it had then been occupied by Alexander the Great and his Ptolemaic successors until Rome took possession in 58 B.C.

While under Ottoman control for centuries, Cyprus had gradually devolved into a British-administered protectorate following the Ottoman defeat in the 1877–1878 Russo-Turkish War. The Greek community on Cyprus first proposed the idea of *énosis* ("union") with the Greek mainland government in 1879. The British initially rejected this plan, but later offered Cyprus to Greece as an inducement to enter World War I on the Allied side. When Greece took more than the stipulated week to decide, however, the British, apparently having second thoughts themselves, withdrew the offer.

The issue reemerged in 1948, when a Cypriot bishop, later known as Archbishop Makarios III, began to promote *énosis* as a way of preventing communism from gaining a foothold on the island. When Britain refused to allow a plebiscite on this issue in 1950, a right wing underground movement known by its Greek acronym EOKA initiated a terrorist campaign against the British presence on the island.

Greece failed in its attempts to have the Cyprus question brought before the United Nations General Assembly, despite the efforts of Archbishop Makarios. As the civil leader of the island's eighty-percent Greek population, he renewed his pleas for *énosis*. At the same time, EOKA stepped up its terrorist efforts against the British. When Britain exiled Makarios in 1956, it was forced to release him soon afterwards due to the fierce response of EOKA. In 1959, the parties agreed to a republic of Cyprus, whose independence was guaranteed by Britain, Greece, and Turkey.

Archbishop Makarios of Cyprus with Cypriot independence fighters Georgios Grivas and Nikos Sampson in 1959.

Makarios was elected president, and a Turkish Cypriot vice-president served under him. Cyprus was admitted to the British Commonwealth and the United Nations one year later. But the possibility of *énosis* still simmered beneath the surface — a dream for the Cypriot Greeks and a nightmare for its Turkish population, not to mention Turkey itself.

The Re-emergence of the Greek Center and Left

This turmoil over Cyprus did not lead, as the rightists had hoped, to a more united support for the government within Greece. In fact, the exile of Makarios turned the majority of Greeks — who were justifiably distrustful of foreign attempts to control Greek affairs anyway — strongly against the British, the United Nations, NATO, and the United States for their failure to back the Greek government on *énosis*. Furthermore, since the rightist government under the premiership of Constantine Karamanlis was correctly perceived as being backed by the United States, this distrust showed itself in a growing support for the re-emerging Left and Center parties — all of which advocated non-alignment.

The most prominent of these parties was the Center Union Party, a coalition of centrists and leftists headed by George Papandreou, the charismatic politician who had negotiated Greece's first post-war government.

In the 1961 elections, Karamanlis' party won fifty-one percent of the vote and 176 seats in parliament, while Papandreou's party took thirty-three percent and 100 seats. The results, however, were highly suspect and led to an increasing and often violent polarization between the supporters of the two parties.

A turning point came with the 1963 murder of Grigoris Lambrakis, a leftist parliamentary deputy, at the hands of extreme rightists. (His death later became an international cause célébre through the novel and Costa-Gavras' film *Z*.) Suspicion that the murder was committed with the tacit complicity of police and the government was one of factors that caused the principled premier, Karamanlis, to step down and call for new elections.

The elections were held in November 1963 under the supervision of the President of the Supreme Court. This time, with no charges of electoral irregularities, Papandreou's party won six more seats than the rightists. The balance of power fell to the leftist EDA party, a legally allowable stand-in for the Communists. Papandreou refused to govern with their support, however, and called for another election — one in which he would eventually gain a workable fifty-five percent majority. Meanwhile, Karamanlis went into self-imposed exile in Paris.

Papandreou immediately embarked on a wide-ranging series of economic and social reforms to better the lot of the ordinary Greek; but these were soon put into jeopardy by the eruption of an all-out civil war in Cyprus between Greek and Turkish nationalists, both of whom advocated a union with their respective mother countries. These hostilities resulted in a near war between Greece and Turkey, as Turkish aircraft bombed the Greek Cypriots. An invasion of the island by the Turks was then prevented by British troops and behind-the-scenes United States intervention. In August of 1964, a United Nations resolution established a cease-fire and sent a peace-keeping force to the island.

In the meantime, King Paul I had died in March 1964 and had been succeeded by his son, Constantine II. The real power, however, was popularly believed to be held by Queen Frederika,

Constantine's mother and a woman greatly disliked by the majority of ordinary Greeks.

As Papandreou moved to establish a political position free of the interference of the United States and Britain, fears of an attempt on his part to deliver Greece to the Communist bloc began to gain widespread currency within rightist circles and within the American and British governments. Thus, plans were made on both the Right and Left to seize power should a crisis arise.

Queen Frederika and King Paul being carried aloft by imprisoned and supposedly repentant Communists during the civil war of 1946–1949.

In May of 1965, a group of leftist army officers called *Aspida* ("shield") were arrested and accused of planning a coup against the government. Andreas Papandreou, the son of the premier, was said to have been connected with the group due to his father's refusal to commit Greece entirely to communism.

Papandreou attempted to purge the army of other officers he suspected of being disloyal in 1965, but the accused had links to the Royalist faction. Constantine's subsequent refusal to sign his directive forced Papandreou to resign as premier and call for a new mandate. Elections, however, were not immediately forthcoming. Constantine instead began appointing a series of non-elected prime ministers to run the country. Papandreou's supporters responded with mass political rallies and, eventually, new elections scheduled for the spring of 1967. Yet they did not take place — nor did a contingency coup d'etat planned by the CIA and Greek army generals to preempt the elections in case of an imminent Papandreou victory.

Instead, a group of unknown army colonels executed a completely unexpected military coup with ruthless efficiency on the morning of April 21, 1967. They would maintain the leadership of Greece for the next seven years.

The Colonels' Junta

The leaders of this military junta came from lower- and middle-class backgrounds, not from the traditionally elite origins of the army's high-ranking officers. They had acted to protect their jobs from a possible Papandreou purge, rather than from any of the lofty ideals preached by the politicians.

Their symbol was a soldier rising Phoenix-like from the flames. Their slogan was "Greece for the Christian Greeks." Their enemies were comprised of any power from both sides of the political spectrum, Monarchists and Communists alike. Martial law was immediately proclaimed. The military, civil service, and judiciary were purged, and political parties were outlawed, along with long hair and mini-skirts. Torture was endemic. Many prominent politicians and their supporters, including the actress Melina Mercouri and the composer Mikis Theordorakis, fled the country to avoid arrest.

In December of 1967, King Constantine II and his family decamped for Rome after failing to arouse the people's support in an ineptly conceived counter-coup. In turn, the man who was emerging as the leader of the junta, Colonel George Papadopoulos, temporarily appointed a regent and then became the regent himself — as well as prime minister and defense and education minister.

While there were many people in the country who plotted his downfall — Alekos Panagoulis (written about so passionately by his lover, the famous journalist Oriana Fallaci in her memoir, *A Man*), for one, actively tried to kill him — there were also many in and outside of the country who welcomed the stability that Papadopoulos and his junta brought to the previously tempestuous and unpredictable politics of the country.

United States Vice-President Spiro Agnew made an official visit to Greece in 1971, bestowing American approval on the regime (and earning even more enmity from the great majority of Greeks). The following year, the United States and the junta signed an agreement allowing the Sixth Fleet, heretofore discretely based in the remote area of Souda Bay in Crete, a base in the high profile port of Piraeus.

In August of 1973, a plebiscite organized by the junta overwhelmingly abolished the monarchy and a "republic" was declared with George Papadopoulos as its president.

But in Greece, perhaps more than anywhere else, pride definitely does go before the fall. Three months after proclaiming a republic, the regime was faced with a serious crisis in the form of a student sit-in at the Athens Polytechnic University. This demonstration quickly escalated into a call to bring down the junta. Papadopoulos, faced with the possibility of the revolt spreading throughout the country, ordered soldiers and tanks into the center of Athens. In the brutal and bloody repression that followed, at least twenty students were killed.

Papadopoulos' tactics so discredited him in Greece and abroad that his fellow officers forced him to resign. A moderate politician named Ghizikas was installed as president, though the real power was tacitly held by General Ioannides, the brutish head of the Greek Secret Police.

By the following summer, such was the distaste for the junta among the populace, as well as in Washington, that most Greeks predicted its imminent downfall daily. In the hopes of restoring patriotic backing for their regime, the Colonels attempted a quick seizure of Cyprus. In July of 1974, they tried to assassinate Archbishop Makarios and replace him with their own man, a former member of EOKA, Nikos Sampson, who would then proclaim *énosis* with Greece.

The student uprising at Athens Polytechnic in November of 1973. The letters hung over the balcony read: "No to the junta."

In the resulting chaos, the Colonels not only lost their own hold on power, but nearly lost Cyprus to a Turkish invasion as well. Makarios survived the assassination attempt and gained the safety of the British base. Meanwhile, the Turkish army invaded Cyprus and quickly took half of the island. The Greek army then attempted to mobilize, but it was clearly so inept and disorganized that the Colonels — pressured by the Americans and other countries whose vacationing nationals were trapped — immediately backed down from war and abandoned their hold on power.

The Return of Karamanlis

On July 24, 1974, former premier Constantine Karamanlis was called back from Paris to form a new government. The country erupted in a paroxysm of relief and joy, greeting him like a fallen hero returned.

On November 17, in the first free elections held since November of 1963, New Democracy, Karamanlis' Right-of-Center party, won the elections by a large majority. It defeated the Center opposition party, the new Socialist PASOK party headed by the charismatic Andreas Papandreou (himself returned from exile in the United States and Paris), and two Communist parties now officially no longer banned: the Moscow-tied KKE and the European-oriented EKE-Interior.

In December of 1974, a new plebiscite on the monarchy was held. Once more, it was overwhelmingly abolished, although this time by a much more believable margin: sixty-nine percent as opposed to the ninety-nine percent tallied under the junta.

Andreas Papandreou being sworn in as prime minister in October of 1981, as then-president Konstantinos Karamanlis attends.

In June of 1975, a new constitution modeled on De Gaulle's Fifth Republic was adopted; but it was quickly denounced by Andreas Papandreou, whose PASOK party was moving increasingly closer to Russia and the Communist bloc. With the idea of forcefully making the point that Greece was a European-oriented country, Karamanlis applied for membership in the EEC.

At about the same time, a shadowy leftist terrorist group, *17 November*, claimed its first victim: the C.I.A. station chief in Athens, Richard Welch. The group would carry out eighteen more self-styled "political" assassinations through 1989 and would later resume their attacks in 2000 — all with the same gun and without a single member of the group being apprehended.

In September of 1977, Karamanlis called for early elections, hoping for a fresh mandate; but his party's margin was considerably reduced, with PASOK reaping the largest gain and becoming the official opposition. Its anti-American, anti-Western stance reflected the beliefs of many Greeks, even those who were not of his political persuasion. Namely, the United States and its allies were the real power behind the rise of the junta and the Turkish attempt to take over Cyprus.

Archbishop Makarios died the same year in Nicosia, the Greek capital of Cyprus. At Vergina in northern Greece, archaeologists discovered the first Macedonian tomb to be found intact, which happened to be the royal burial of Philip II, father of Alexander the Great. For a brief moment, this latter event would focus the country's pride and attention on another part of Greece thought to be threatened by foreign interests: Macedonia.

In 1980, the aging and infirm Karamanlis stood for the heretofore ceremonial post of president, with the hope of maintaining stability in the country while allowing for free and fair elections between the increasingly polarized Right, Left, and Center parties. Upon winning the presidential post by a small margin, Karamanlis resigned as prime minister. The New Democracy's chosen successor to the post was the foreign minister, George Rallis.

Three weeks later, Greece signed a Treaty of Accession to join the Common Market; but in the ensuing debate on ratification, PASOK and the Communist parties walked out.

The Papandreou Years

On the first day of 1981, Greece became the tenth member of the EEC — a hasty move for which the country was not thought to be either politically or economically ready. However, the membership was perceived by most interested parties as the quickest insurance against another coup d'état.

Shortly thereafter, the notorious Queen Frederika died in exile. To a storm of protest by the great majority, Rallis' government allowed her to be buried beside her husband, Paul I, at the royal palace outside Athens. Constantine and others attended the ceremonies, but departed the country the same day.

Such a blatant misreading of the general public's mood would be one of many factors that would give Andreas Papandreou's PASOK party, calling for *allaghí* ("change"), a huge margin of victory in the October 1981 general elections. Thus, his was the first Socialist government in Greek history. As minister of culture, he named his close friend and longtime party stalwart, Melina Mercouri.

Declaring a "Greece for the Greeks" — an utterance uncomfortably close to the junta's "Greece for the Christian Greeks" — Papandreou immediately called for the United States to remove its bases, demanded a renegotiation of the EEC agreement, and threatened to withdraw from NATO. At the same time, he began strengthening Greece's ties with the radical Arab states and the Eastern bloc countries.

Over the next three tumultuous years, Papandreou: refused to support Common Market sanctions against Poland; signed an agreement with Turkey not to engage in provocative acts; forged an agreement with the United States for a limited use of bases in the country; assumed the presidency of the EEC; vetoed Spain and Portugal's bid to join the organization; and brokered a meeting in Crete between France's Socialist president, François Mitterand, and Libya's Muammar al-Qaddafi.

In March of 1985, Papandreou persuaded Karamanlis to resign and call for new presidential elections to be held, promising to support him. However, he swung his support instead to Christos Sarzetakis, the investigating magistrate in the murder of leftist deputy Lambrakis. Defeated, Karamanlis again left in exile as his New Democracy party refused to recognize the elections.

In the same year, the Macedonian capital of Thessaloniki celebrated the 2,300-year anniversary of its founding by Philip II's son-in-law, Cassander. However, a planned exhibit of priceless church relics and manuscripts from Mt. Athos was canceled by the church for fear that Papandreou's government would nationalize the items once they were outside of the autonomous monastic republic.

In June of 1985, PASOK again won the general elections, though with a slightly reduced majority. In the same month, Shi'ite terrorists easily boarded and hijacked a TWA 747 at the Athens airport — an event that sparked international uproar because of Papandreou's ties to and tolerance of Arab states known to support terrorism.

On November 10, however, the Papandreou government signed a defense and industrial cooperation pact with the United States; the following January, it announced that it was ready to reopen negotiations over the United States bases in Greece. Shortly after that, a contract was signed with General Dynamics to purchase forty fighter planes.

In 1987, the Orthodox Church's fears of the PASOK government proved well founded, as the Socialist-dominated parliament caused a huge controversy by passing a law allowing it to confiscate 325,000 acres of church land. Meanwhile, relations between the United States and Greece continued apace with PASOK denouncing the United States for its military aid to Turkey; shortly afterwards, though, it accepted its own package of five hundred M48 tanks. The following year, after a bus had been bombed as a protest to the bases, the United States accused Greece of working in concert with the Abu Nidal terrorist group.

The heady ride in power of Papandreou's party was soon to come to an end — events would prove that absolute power both corrupts and is the ultimate aphrodisiac.

In November of 1988, the Greek banker George Koskotas was charged in a scheme to skim $210 million from government pension funds deposited in the Bank of Crete. He had purchased the institution along with seven magazines, a newspaper, soccer club, radio station, and various other holdings in a whirlwind series of acquisitions — one that began after his return to Greece from the United States in 1982. Apparently warned of his pending arrest, he fled Greece but was later imprisoned in Salem, Massachusetts. Connections to the upper echelons of the Papandreou government were assumed but had not yet been proven.

The now seventy-year-old Prime Minister Papandreou enthralled the world press by appearing at the EEC summit in Rhodes with his half-as-old paramour, Dimitra Liani, whom he had met when she was an airline hostess on one of his flights. Papandreou was concurrently seeking a divorce from his American-born wife, Margaret.

In a *Time* magazine interview shortly thereafter, Koskotas implicated Papandreou and his ministers in a scheme to use state revenues and pension money to finance PASOK political contingencies, as well as to fill their own private bank accounts in Switzerland.

Papandreou's divorce in June of 1989 was followed two days later by new general elections. This time, the opposition New Democracy headed by Constantine Mitsotakis won the election but missed an absolute majority by six seats. New Democracy and Synaspismos, the new Communist "alliance" party, consequently formed a three-month coalition government. Its sole purpose would be to investigate the Koskotas affair and encourage a national *kathársis*.

Papandreou married Dimitra Liani the following month. In August, after trying to pass off Yugoslavian corn as Greek produce in order to gain EC subsidies, several PASOK ministers were indicted for fraud. The debate on the Koskotas scandal was scheduled to open in the parliament in September; just hours before it opened, the Greek terrorist organization *17 November* gunned down parliamentary deputy Pavlos Bakoyiannis, Mitsotakis' son-in-law and the principal architect of the coalition government. Two days later, on September 28, the parliament indicted Papandreou for illegal phone tapping, bribe taking, and breach of faith as prime minister of the country.

In the new general elections held on November 15, Papandreou's PASOK party nevertheless gained two seats. New Democracy fell two votes short of an absolute majority. A compromise, "ecumenical" government was then agreed upon by the three major parties, until a new election could be held.

In June of 1990, with Papandreou and other party members still under an indictment, New Democracy finally won a majority in the general election. Constantine Mitsotakis became the prime minister, and Constantine Karamanlis was again elected president.

The following year, several important events took place: Greece celebrated the $2,500^{th}$ anniversary of democracy; Papandreou and others were tried in the Koskotas embezzlement scandal; and, under a new agreement, the United States closed its air base in Athens, while retaining two on Crete. President George Bush also traveled to Greece in the first visit by a United States head of state since Eisenhower in 1959.

The long-simmering Macedonian crisis suddenly erupted in 1992, as an independent Republic of Macedonia was declared in southeastern Yugoslavia and immediately recognized by Bulgaria. In Greece, particularly in its northern capital of Thessaloniki, massive rallies were held in protest — a response to the long-held belief that this act was merely a prelude to a Balkan states' claim to all of Greek Macedonia and its coveted outlet to the Aegean.

Meanwhile, Papandreou was acquitted in the embezzlement scandal, although Koskotas and other ministers were found guilty on related charges. Municipal by-elections of approximately the same time in Athens resulted in a huge victory for PASOK. Its followers thus remained not only loyal to Papandreou and their party, but displayed their conviction that all of the charges had been trumped up by the Right with the aid of the United States.

The following year, as differences between Greece and the former Yugoslavian Republic of Macedonia remained unresolved over the use of the name "Macedonia," Andreas Papandreou was once again elected prime minister. His PASOK party took 46.7 percent of the vote over New Democracy, prompting its leader, former Prime Minister Constantine Mitsotakis, to resign.

In February of 1994, Greece closed its border with Yugoslavia and imposed a trade blockade that it said it would not lift until "Macedonia" — dubbed "FYROM" ("Former Republic of Yugoslavia") by Greece — changed its name, flag, and constitution. This state of affairs would last until September 1995, when both sides agreed at the United Nations to attempt to reach a compromise.

There was also tension with Albania, whose native-born Greek extremists under the "Northern Epirus Liberation Front" agitated to expand the Greek province of Epirus into Albania proper, and killed two Albanian border police in the process.

Then, on May 19, 1994 — as if the above were not enough for the ever-contentious Papandreou government and its habit of finding common enemies to take people's minds off internal woes — Greece unilaterally reopened old wounds and tensions with Turkey by declaring a "Day of Remembrance" to commemorate the Turkish massacre of Greeks in 1919, which it referred to as "Turkish genocide." That this commemoration fell on the day when the Turks had a national holiday celebrating Ataturk's counterstrike against the Greek forces at Smyrna (Izmir) exacerbated the provocation even further. Only recently has this state of tension abated, thanks to efforts by the Greek and Turkish foreign ministers and the United States-based East-West Institute.

The quai at Smyrna, September 13, 1922, as the Turkish army pushes the Greek forces and civilians into the sea.

In November of 1994, the volatile situation was further inflamed when the international Law of the Sea Conference agreed to allow countries to extend their coastal waters from six to twelve miles — a potentially catastrophic license for disaster in the Greek-Turkish Aegean with its complex intermingling of coastlines and islets only a few miles or even meters apart. Following Greece's ratification of the new law in June of 1995, there were several incidents that would bring the two countries to the brink of war.

Minister of Culture Melina Mercouri died in March of 1994, and her campaign to have the Elgin Marbles returned from the British Museum was left unresolved. The following month, King Constantine had his Greek citizenship revoked and his royal property taken over by the Greek government.

The tension with Albania momentarily abated in 1995 as four of the five ethnic Greeks, jailed for eight years for extremist activities, were released. Then, Greek border guards shot an Albanian, and tempers flared anew. The Cyprus situation also continued to simmer with talk of consideration for EU membership. Greece speculated once more about *énosis*, while Turkey threatened full annexation of the island if this issue was not settled beforehand. At the same time, Greece continued to block Turkey's possible accession to the EU, unless the Cyprus question was resolved to its own satisfaction.

All of these issues, however, were soon relegated to the back burner on November 20 by the sudden admittance of the 76-year-old Andreas Papandreou to the Onassis Heart Center in Athens. His ailments were manifold and included pneumonia and ensuing secondary infections, as well as heart, lung, and kidney complications. He was subsisting on life support systems by the end of the year, when a Turkish fighter plane, testing the readiness of the Greek air defense system, crashed in the sea near Mytilene (Lesbos).

The Post-Papandreou Era

After stubbornly trying to run the country from his hospital bed, Papandreou finally resigned in January of 1996. Though he had at last heeded the advice of his eldest son George, the PASOK minister of education, Papandreou nevertheless retained his hold on the party presidency, continuing to mesmerize PASOK politicians as he lay in the hospital like a dying but still-dangerous cobra. Former Minister of Industry Costas Simitis assumed the premiership with promises to reduce the bloated Socialist budget and bring the country in line with EU monetary requirements. Although Papandreou was able to leave the hospital in March and hang onto the party leadership, he eventually succumbed to his illness and died in June.

At the ensuing party conference, his son, George Papandreou, backed the election of Simitis to the party presidency. In a general election in September, PASOK won by a comfortable twelve-seat margin, and Simitis was installed as prime minister for another four years.

Tensions with Turkey reached a boiling point in January of 1996, when Turkish journalists planted a Turkish flag on Imia, a tiny islet in the Dodecanese used by a Greek to graze his goats. As the two countries' troops and warships squared off against one another at various points along the length of their borders, the United States quietly stepped in and defused the situation. The islet was returned to Greece and the goat herder.

The fact that Simitis did the previously unthinkable by publicly thanking the United States for its intervention was considered an encouraging sign that a less extreme, post-Papandreou foreign policy was definitely in effect. One month later, Hillary and Chelsea Clinton arrived to light the flame for the 1996 Olympic Games.

The tension with Turkey again reached crisis proportions in August of 1996, when Turkish troops on Cyprus fatally shot two Greek Cypriots who had protested the division of the island. On the other hand, in December of that year, a meeting between Greek and Turkish businessmen in Athens indicated that something else was quietly going on behind the scenes.

In the meantime, the mysterious terrorist group *17 November* had resurfaced in February with a rocket attack on the United States embassy in Athens; and, in April, it attempted to kill a member of the Greek Supreme Court by bombing his apartment. This year also saw Egyptian Islamic terrorists kill eighteen Greek tourists in a bus in Cairo, believing them to be Israelis.

In 1997, Simitis' tight economic policies began to pay off in the form of an inflation rate below five percent and an on-target (but barely) projection to meet EU currency convergence requirements. However, these austere policies provoked a large number of public demonstrations against the economic restrictions and other areas of discontent. The year was marked by a series of strikes, most prominently by farmers, teachers, and garbage collectors — not to mention the general strikes that followed the publication of a 1998 budget announcing more government spending cuts.

Relations with Turkey continued to be strained as the Turkish government, attempting to divert its own peoples' attention away from troubles with Islamic and Kurdish extremists, kept up its hostile accusations and threats of war. Greece answered in kind by continuing to impede Turkey's efforts to join the EU.

On the brighter side, Greece's memories of its presumptuous, highhanded failure to win the rights for the 1996 Olympic Games were wiped away by the acceptance of its bid to host them in 2004.

As anti-government strikes continued and a new terrorist group called "Arsonists of Conscience" began torching vehicles around Greece in 1998, the incursion of refugees from other hot spots — particularly Albania, Iraq, and Pakistan — reached epidemic proportions. An estimated 600,000 to 800,000 illegal immigrants now resided in the country.

In April, the Jewish Center in Athens was bombed; Greece assumed the presidency of the Council of Europe; and Constantine Karamanlis died of cardiac arrest at the age of 91, having lived long enough to see his nephew, Costas Karamanlis, elected to the presidency of his old New Democracy party. Among the elder Karamanlis' many pungent comments, the *Athens Daily News* quoted the following: "When I first went into politics, I thought Greeks were very individualistic and poor at working collectively because they were poor. Being poor makes you cunning and conniving. So I thought, well, I'll make them richer. To some extent, I did. But nothing changed. . . ."

In July, Greek Prime Minister Costas Simitis met secretly with his Turkish counterpart at a NATO summit in Madrid and signed an agreement on principles for normalizing relations. But one of the agreement's points, which affirmed each country's legitimate interests in the Aegean, set off a universal storm of protest in Greece. All sides of the political spectrum accused Simitis of giving in to the Turks.

This outrage was quickly swept under the table by two other crises during the same month. The first involved mounting tension on Cyprus as the twenty-fourth anniversary of Turkey's invasion was commemorated by the Greek Cypriots with five minutes of prayer and silence, the tolling of church bells, and an eerie wailing of air raid sirens. This commemoration was held against the backdrop of Greek-Cypriot plans to deploy S-300 anti-aircraft missiles around an air base recently enlarged to accommodate the landing of Greek air force fighter planes. Meanwhile, the Turks were holding maneuvers of their own fleet north of the island.

The second crisis immediately took precedence, however, as NATO began bombing the Serbs for having invaded Kosovo. Believing themselves forever joined with the Serbs against the Moslems in the heroic stand against the Ottoman forces at Kosovo in 1389, the Greek people were incensed by the military campaign. Greek newspapers quickly attacked the decision, with most opining that United States President Clinton had ordered the action in order to divert attention away from his affair with Monica Lewinsky. Some eighty percent of the Greeks later said they believed that Clinton, not Serbian president Slobodan Milosevic, should be tried as a war criminal for his actions in the area.

In October, despite these threats from outside the country, public dissatisfaction with Simitis' economic policies led to a major defeat for his party in local elections. Costas Karamanlis' New Democracy party took a majority of both the number of prefectures and municipal positions held.

The year ended with a hopeful meeting between the newly-elected president of the Former Yugoslav Republic of Macedonia (FYROM) and an envoy from Simitis. On this day, meetings were conducted between the FYROM government and Greek businessmen, and a Greek Cultural Week was initiated in the FYROM capital of Skopje.

Nevertheless, the presence of NATO peacekeeping forces in FYROM and the continuing bombardment of the Serbs by NATO planes meant that the area would be a target for Greek protests throughout the upcoming year.

In January of 1999, the port authority in Thessaloniki and the Greek anti-terrorist bureau detained large shipments of arms destined for Skopje on the pretext that some were without the proper labeling and shipping permits. There were continuing anti-bombing demonstrations throughout the following months — particularly in March, when some fifteen thousand protesters marched on the British and United States embassies in Athens. The Greek press simultaneously engaged in oneupmanship in their attacks on the United States. Together, they likened the bombing to Hitler's *blitzkrieg*, saying that it was to protect the drug trade in Kosovo, just as the United States had done in FYROM, Pakistan, Afghanistan, Turkey, and Panama; and they hinted at darker plots to subsequently take over Thrace on the pretext of protecting the Muslim minority there.

Meanwhile, the February 1999 arrest of the fugitive Turkish Kurd leader, Abdullah Ocalan, precipitated a grand scandal reminiscent of the turbulent regime of the elder Papandreou. Suspicions of complicity by the Greek government and its National Intelligence Agency in either the arrest and/or the ability of Ocalan to elude capture for so long led to the firing of the Secret Service Chief and a reshuffling of government ministers by Prime Minister Simitis. The most significant of these changes was the replacement of Greece's controversial and militant foreign minister, Theodoros Pangalos, with the education minister, George Papandreou. The latter was said to have demanded of Simitis that those responsible for the Ocalan scandal be punished.

Against a background of the continuing vilification of NATO and the United States by the Greek populace and press, the holding of anti-war concerts to raise money for Serbian relief, and the efforts of municipalities in collecting food and clothing to send to Belgrade, Simitis' government managed to resist a temptation to climb wholeheartedly aboard the bandwagon. Instead, there were moments when its representatives even dared to criticize Milosevic in public for causing the tragedy of Kosovo with his policy of ethnic cleansing. And in the meantime, the government continued quiet, behind-the-scenes negotiations on all fronts to achieve stability in the area.

In April of 1999, after seven long years of tension, the Greek and FYROM governments signed an agreement on a mutually acceptable name for the new country: the "Republic of Macedonia-Skopje" (RMS).

In July of the same year, the Greeks became instrumental in mediating a withdrawal of Serbian forces from Kosovo; and

Greece and Turkey announced that they had agreed to high-level talks on topics ranging from trade and tourism to immigration and security — all under the umbrella of promoting widespread stability in the Balkans.

But it would take three natural catastrophes to seal the deal and accomplish the most to ease decades of distrust among the peoples of both countries. A massive earthquake, killing some eighteen thousand people, struck a densely-populated area just to the southeast of Istanbul in mid-July 1999. With the agreement of the previous month in place, the Greek government responded by being the first foreign government to send aid and to have specialists help find people trapped in the rubble.

In September, a smaller earthquake struck a suburb of Athens. Turkey immediately responded with aid of its own. Finally, but one month later, a second quake devastated Turkey, and Greece quickly rushed in with more aid.

While these seismic events cannot be called fortuitous due to the terrible destruction they wrought, it cannot be denied that there could have been nothing more dramatic to prove to the people of both countries their common humanity and their need for each other.

Following President Clinton's brief and protest-ridden visit to both Turkey and Athens in November of 1999, the Greek and Turkish governments took even larger steps towards a complete rapprochement between the two nations. Tough negotiations ensued at a European Council meeting in Helsinki in December. Eventually, Turkey dropped its demands that Cyprus' candidacy for EU membership be contingent upon a resolution of its status vis-à-vis Greece and Turkey. In return, Greece removed its objections to Turkey's EU candidacy.

The year ended with George Papandreou making the first visit by a Greek foreign minister to Turkey since 1962 — one that yielded a series of "confidence-building measures" with the Turkish foreign minister in Ankara. These agreements covered tourism, the environment, investment protection, illegal migration, and a coordinated effort to deal with terrorism, organized crime, and money laundering.

The year 2000 began with PASOK and New Democracy running neck and neck in the polls, and Prime Minister Simitis undecided about when and whether to hold early elections before the end of his four-year term in September. Further meetings were scheduled between the Greek and Turkish foreign ministers, this time in Athens.

In 2004, Athens will host the Olympic Games for the first time since they were re-inaugurated there in 1896 — a time when Greece was just beginning the far from completed process of forging its own identity in the modern world.

INDEX

Forthcoming Illustrated Histories
from Hippocrene Books
FALL 2000

France: An Illustrated History
Lisa Neal

Encompassing more than 500,000 years from primordial times to the 21st century, French history is a vast body run through by manifold, and often turbulent, currents. This volume provides a succinct panorama of these cultural, political, and social currents, as well as concise analyses of their origins and effects. Complemented by 50 illustrations and maps, this text is an invaluable addition to the library of the traveler, the student, and the history enthusiast.

150 pages • 5 x 7 • 50 b/w photos/illus./maps
• $14.95hc • 0-7818-0835-9 • W • (105)

Korea: An Illustrated History from Ancient Times to 1945
David Rees

Koreans call their country *Choson*, which is familiarly translated as "The Land of the Morning Calm." From the time of the legendary Tan-Gun in the third millennium B.C. until the middle of the twentieth century, however, Korea was forced to weather many military and political storms. This volume concisely depicts these political and social events, as well as Korea's profound spiritual and cultural heritage—all enriched by 55 illustrations and maps.

150 pages • 5 x 7 • 50 b/w photos/illus./maps • $14.95hc • 0-7818-0785-9 • W • (152)

Poland: An Illustrated History
Iwo Cyprian Pogonowski

Poland's remarkable quest for representative government, the oldest in modern Europe, is presented against the backdrop of a millennium of history rich in cultural, political, and social events. These topics—complemented with Polish art, literature, music, architecture, and traditions—are knowledgably described in this concise volume, which further offers more than 50 photos, illustrations, and maps.

150 pages • 5 x 7 • 50 b/w photos/illus./maps • $14.95hc • 0-7818-0757-3 • W • (404)

Spain: An Illustrated History
Fred James Hill

This concise, illustrated history explores the remarkable history of Spain—a thriving center of Islamic civilization until its eventual conquest by Catholic kings—from the first millennium B.C. to the 21st century. With its succinct portrayal of the country's political and social history, along with the concomitant cultural developments and achievements, this volume is perfect for the traveler, student, and history enthusiast.

150 pages • 5 x 7 • 50 b/w photos/illus./maps • $14.95hc • 0-7818-0836-7 • W • (113)

Other Illustrated Histories from Hippocrene Books. . .

The Celtic World: An Illustrated History
Patrick Lavin

From the valleys of Bronze Age Urnfielders to the works of 20th century Irish-American literary greats Mary Higgins Clark and Seamus Heaney, Patrick Lavin guides the reader on an entertaining and informative journey through 185 captivating pages of Celtic history, culture, and tradition. Complemented by 50 illustrations and maps, this concise yet insightful survey is a convenient reference guide for both the traveler and scholar.

185 pages • 5 x 7 • 50 b/w illus./maps
• $14.95hc • 0-7818-0731-X • W • (582)

England: An Illustrated History
Henry Weisser

English history is a rich and complex subject that has had a major influence upon the development of the language, laws, institutions, practices and ideas of the United States and many other countries throughout the world. Just how did all of this originate over the centuries in this pleasant, green kingdom? This concise, illustrated volume traces the story from England's most distant past to the present day, highlighting important political and social developments as well as cultural achievements.

166 pages • 5 x 7 • 50 b/w illus./maps
• $11.95hc • 0-7818-0751-4 • W • (446)

Ireland: An Illustrated History
Henry Weisser

Erin go bragh! While it is easy to appreciate the natural beauty of Ireland, the Emerald Isle's history is also a rich and complex subject of study. Spanning prehistoric and Celtic Ireland to modern times, this concise, illustrated volume examines the people, religion, social changes, and politics that have evolved into the tradition of modern Ireland.

166 pages • 5 x 7 • 50 b/w illus./maps
• $11.95hc • 0-7818-0693-3 • W • (782)

Israel: An Illustrated History
David C. Gross

Israel has always been a major player on the world stage. This concise, illustrated volume offers the reader an informative, panoramic view of this remarkable land, from biblical days to the 21st century. With topics exploring art, literature, sculpture, music, science, politics, religion and more, here is a wonderful gift book for travelers, students, or anyone seeking to expand their knowledge of Israeli history, culture, and heritage.

160 pages • 5 x 7 • 50 b/w illus./maps
• $11.95hc • 0-7818-0756-5 • W • (24)

Mexico: An Illustrated History
Michael Burke

This convenient historical guide traces Mexico from the peasant days of the Olmecs to the late 20th century. With over 150 pages and 50 illustrations, the reader discovers how events of Mexico's past have left an indelible mark on the politics, economy, culture, spirit, and growth of this country and its people.

183 pages • 5 x 7 • 50 b/w illus.
• $11.95hc • 0-7818-0690-9 • W • (585)

Poland in World War II: An Illustrated Military History
Andrew Hempel

This illustrated history is a concise presentation of the Polish military war effort in World War II, intermingled with factual human-interest stories and 50 black-and-white photos and illustrations.

117 pages • 5 x 7 • 50 b/w illus.
• $11.95hc • 0-7818-0758-1 • W • (541)

Russia: An Illustrated History
Joel Carmichael

Encompassing one-sixth of the earth's land surface—the equivalent of the whole North American continent—Russia is the largest country in the world. Renowned historian Joel Carmichael presents Russia's rich and expansive past—upheaval, reform, social change, growth—in an easily accessible and concentrated volume. From the Tatar's reign to modern-day Russia, the book spans seven centuries of cultural, social and political events.

252 pages • 5 x 7 • 50 b/w illus.
• $14.95hc • 0-7818-0689-5 • W • (781)

Prices subject to change without notice. **To purchase Hippocrene Books** contact your local bookstore, call (718) 454-2366, or write to: HIPPOCRENE BOOKS, 171 Madison Avenue, New York, NY 10016. Please enclose check or money order, adding $5.00 shipping (UPS) for the first book and $.50 for each additional book.